Training Radical Leaders

TRAINING RADICAL LEADERS

How to Multiply Leaders in a Discipleship Movement Using Ten
Proven Bible Studies

Daniel B Lancaster

Lightkeeper Books
Nashville, Tennessee

Training Radical Leaders/ Daniel B Lancaster

ISBN 978-19389204-0-0

In Memory of Tom

CONTENTS

PREFACE

My prayer is this book will strengthen your walk with God. May you draw closer to Jesus every day and be filled with the Spirit. May you have a deep sense in your spirit that God loves you and will help you defeat any fear.

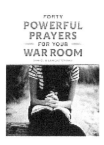

I have included several bonus gifts that I believe will be a blessing to you. The free *Making Disciples Bonus Pak* which includes three resources to help you pray powerful prayers:

- *100 Promises Audio Version*
- *40 Discipleship Quotes*
- *40 Powerful Prayers*

All are suitable for framing. To download your free *Making Disciples Bonus Pak,* CLICK HERE

I've also included an excerpt from my bestselling book *Powerful Jesus in the War Room*. God has blessed many through this book and I wanted to give you a chance to "try before you buy." To order *Powerful Jesus in the War Room*, CLICK HERE.

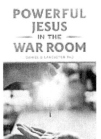

If you like the book, please leave a review. Your feedback will help other believers find this book easier and encourage me in my calling to write practical, powerful books to encourage, equip, and empower Christians throughout the world.

Every Blessing,

Daniel B Lancaster

Nashville, Tennessee — January 2014

ACKNOWLEDGMENTS

Every training book is a compilation of lessons learned in life. The Follow Jesus Training Series is no exception. I owe a debt of gratitude to many people who have trained me, so I could train others.

Several friends in Southeast Asia worked side-by-side with me to develop these leadership training materials. Thank you Gilbert David, Jeri Whitfield, Craig Garrison, Steve Smith, Neill Mims, and Woody & Lynn Thingpen for your insights, support, and help. We have walked this journey together many years.

Several spiritual leaders have significantly influenced my life and I would like to thank them. Dr. Ricky Paris taught me how to seek God with all my heart. Gaylon Lane, L.D. Baxley, and Tom Popelka modeled unconditional love and spiritual leadership during a rough part of my pilgrimage. Dr. Elvin McCann encouraged the mission fire God has placed inside me. Rev. Nick Olson showed me how to be a man of strategy and integrity. Dr. Ben Smith introduced Jesus to me and has remained a confidant since then. Dr. Roy Fish cast a vision for multiplication of disciples early in my ministry. Rev. Ron Capps taught me "the greatest leader is the greatest servant." Thank you everyone for training me as a leader, so I could train others.

Tom Wells served as worship leader at Highland Fellowship, the second church we planted. A gifted musician and dear friend, Tom and I spent many coffees together talking about the eight pictures of Christ. He helped me develop the simple method of finding out personality used in *Training Radical Leaders*. We organized the church and planned ministries based on the eight pictures of Christ. We also provided consulting services to local churches regarding church health. Though you are now with the Lord, Tom, know your work goes on, we remember you, and we miss you much.

I also give special thanks to David and Jill Shanks who contributed toward this project. Their generosity enabled countless believers in Asia to grow stronger in discipleship, leadership, and church planting. The line in heaven will be long, waiting to say "Thank you."

Finally, my family offers this book as a gift to yours. Holli, my wife, and my children, Jeff, Zach, Karis, and Zane, all sacrificed and supported this effort to develop passionate, spiritual leaders and bring healing to the nations.

INTRODUCTION

God granted our family the privilege of starting two churches in America. The first church was in Hamilton, Texas, the rural county seat of one of the poorest counties in Texas. The memories of how God provided for that mighty band of believers to build a 200-seat church building debt-free amid economic hard times still warms hearts today. God changed all of our lives when He remembered Hamilton.

We started our second church plant in Lewisville, Texas. I had spent my junior high and high school years in Lewisville, a progressive suburb in the Dallas and Ft. Worth area. My home church, Lakeland Baptist, sponsored the church plant and generously supported us financially, emotionally, and spiritually. We were the eighteenth church they had planted in the area. Because of our previous experience as church planters, the pastor asked us to start the church without a core group, relying mainly on door-to-door appeals.

Two months into the church plant, I developed significant pain throughout my body and suffered from severe fatigue. Doctors identified the disease as lupus on the same day our fourth child was born. Later tests altered the diagnosis to ankylosing spondylitis – an arthritic disease that melds the spine, rib cage, and hip joints. High-powered painkillers gave some relief, but also made me drowsy. I could work two hours each day at most and spent the rest of the time resting and praying.

This period in our ministry was a "dark night of the soul." The fatigue and pain limited everything. Although I was very ill, we felt like God was still calling us to start the church. We asked Him to release us, but He responded by reminding us that His grace was sufficient. We felt like God had left us, but His love never wavered. We questioned our call, but He continued to draw us closer to Himself and give us hope. We wondered if God was punishing us for some unknown sin, but He filled us with faith that He would save lost people and return them to His family. Our dream of going to the mission field one day slowly faded and eventually disappeared.

How would you invest your time if you could only work two hours a day in a new church start? God led us to focus on developing leaders. I learned how to spend one hour with a person at lunch and leave them with a strategic plan for the coming month, usually written on a napkin! A multiplication ethos of training others, who in turn trained others, developed. We helped people find out how God had "wired" them and how to abide in Christ in practical ways. Many adults and children entered the Kingdom, despite the physical suffering we faced.

Three years into my illness, we started a new medicine that changed our night into day. The pain and fatigue became manageable. Instead of returning to the old model of the pastor doing everything, we persisted on the same path of developing leaders. Four years after starting the church, I took a vision trip to Southeast Asia with a friend. When I stepped off the plane in a foreign land, God spoke to my heart and said, "You are home." I called my wife that night and she confirmed God had spoken the same call to both of us. A year later, we sold everything we had, packed up our family of four, and moved to Southeast Asia.

We worked in a closed country and began to make disciples. We asked God to give us three men and three women we could pour our lives into, following Jesus' example of focusing on Peter, James, and John. God answered our prayer and sent us people we could come alongside and train, like Barnabas trained Paul. As we trained more and more people to follow Jesus, they started many new groups, some of which became churches. As they grew, groups and churches soon wrestled with the need for more and better leaders.

The country where we ministered also suffered from a leadership vacuum and sparse leadership development. We began an extensive study of how Jesus trained the disciples as leaders. We taught those lessons to our national friends and made an interesting discovery; making disciples and training leaders are two sides of the same coin. "Making disciples" describes the beginning of the journey and "training leaders" describes continuing the journey. We also discovered that the more we mirrored Jesus, the more reproducible our training became.

The reproducible lessons we taught leaders comprise this training manual. Jesus is the greatest leader of all time and lives in His followers. As we follow Him, we become better leaders. May God bless you as a leader and the people you influence through this training manual. Many leaders have successfully trained generations of leaders with these materials and we pray God's blessing on your life as you do the same.

PART I

NUTS AND BOLTS

JESUS' STRATEGY

Jesus' strategy to reach the nations involves five tactics: Be strong in God, share the gospel, make disciples, start groups that lead to churches, and develop leaders. While each tactic stands alone, they join to create a synergistic process. The material in *Follow Jesus Training* enables trainers to be a catalyst for a church-planting movement among their people, simply by following Jesus.

Follow Jesus Training begins with *Making Radical Disciples* and the first four tactics in Jesus' strategy. Disciples learn how to pray, obey Jesus' commands, and walk in the power of the Holy Spirit (Be Strong in God). Disciples then discover how to join God where He is working and share their testimony – a powerful weapon in spiritual warfare. Next, they learn how to share the gospel and invite people back to God's family (Share the Gospel). Completing the course provides leaders with the tools to start a small group, cast a vision for multiplication, and a plan to reach their community (Start Groups).

Growing disciples expressed two felt needs as we trained and coached them. Emerging leaders wondered how to grow as spiritual leaders and what steps were necessary to transition from a group to a church. Because the tactics in Jesus' strategy are not sequential, some disciples asked for leadership training and then church-planting training. Other disciples reversed that order. As a result, we began to offer two extra training seminars to disciples who used *Making Radical Disciples* and were faithful to train others.

Starting Radical Churches aids existing churches in starting new groups and churches – the fourth tactic in Jesus' strategy. Few leaders have started a church and one frequent mistake made is copying the structure of their current church in the new church plant. This approach almost guarantees meager results. Starting Radical Churches avoids this mistake by training disciples how to follow the eight commands of Christ that the early Church obeyed in Acts 2. The group works through practical applications of each command and develops a church covenant together. If the group senses God's leading, the seminar ends with a ceremony of celebration and dedication as a new church.

Training Radical Leaders helps leaders train others to become passionate, spiritual leaders – the fifth tactic in Jesus' strategy. A key ingredient in church-planting movements is leadership development. The seminar shows leaders the process Jesus used to train leaders and the seven leadership qualities of Jesus, the greatest leader of all time. Leaders discover their personality type and ways to help people with different personalities work together. Finally, leaders develop a "Jesus Plan" based on twelve ministry principles Jesus gave the disciples in Luke 10. The seminar closes with leaders sharing their "Jesus Plan" and praying with one another. Leaders commit to coaching one another and developing new leaders.

Both *Starting Radical Churches* and *Training Radical Leaders* train disciples how to imitate Jesus' ministry and method. Trainers give leaders reproducible tools they can master and share with others. *Follow Jesus Training* is not a course to learn, but a way to live. For more than two thousand years, God has blessed and changed countless lives through the simplicity of following His Son. Believers have followed Jesus' strategy and seen whole cultures transformed. May God do the same in your life and among the people you train to follow Jesus.

TRAINING LEADERS

Training Radical Leaders builds on the first course, *Making Radical Disciples*, and helps those who have started disciple groups grow as leaders and multiply more groups.

TRAINING RESULTS

After completing this training seminar, learners can:

- Teach other leaders ten core leadership lessons.
- Train other leaders using a reproducible process modeled by Jesus.
- Identify different personality types and help people work together as a team.
- Develop a strategic plan to engage the spiritually lost in their community and multiply new groups.
- Understand how to lead a church-planting movement.

TRAINING PROCESS

Each leadership training session follows the same format, based on how Jesus trained the disciples as leaders. A generic lesson outline follows, with suggested time-periods.

PRAISE

Sing two choruses or hymns together (or more as time allows).

(10 minutes)

PROGRESS

A leader shares about the progress in their ministry since the last time the leaders met. The group prays for the leader and his or her ministry.

(10 minutes)

PROBLEM

The trainer introduces a common leadership problem, explaining it with a story or personal illustration.

(5 minutes)

PLAN

The trainer teaches leaders a simple leadership lesson that gives insight and skills into solving the leadership problem.

(20 minutes)

PRACTICE

Leaders divide into groups of four and practice the leadership training method by discussing the lesson they have just learned, including:

- Progress made in this leadership area.
- Problems faced in this leadership area.
- Plans to improve in the next 30 days based on the leadership lesson.
- A skill they will practice in the next 30 days based on the leadership lesson.

Leaders stand and repeat the memory verse ten times together, six times reading the Bible, and four times from memory.

(30 minutes)

PRAYER

Groups of four share prayer concerns and pray for each other.

(10 minutes)

ENDING

Most sessions end with a learning activity to help leaders apply the leadership lesson to their own context.

(15 minutes)

TRAINING PRINCIPLES

Helping others develop as leaders is exciting and demanding work. Contrary to popular opinion, leaders are made, not born. For more leaders to emerge, leadership development must be intentional and systematic. Some people mistakenly believe leaders become leaders based on their personality. A quick survey of successful mega-church pastors in America, however, reveals pastors with many different personalities. When we follow Jesus, we follow the greatest leader of all time, and develop as leaders ourselves.

Rising leaders need a balanced approach to leadership development. A balanced approach includes work on knowledge, character, skills, and motivation. A person needs all four ingredients to be an effective leader. Without knowledge, wrong assumptions and misunderstandings misdirect the leader. Without character, a leader will make moral and spiritual mistakes that hamper the mission. Without necessary skills, the leader will continuously reinvent the wheel or use outdated methods. Finally, a leader with knowledge, character, and skill, but no motivation cares only for the status quo and preserving his or her position.

Leaders must learn the key tools needed to get the job done.

After spending significant time in prayer, every leader needs a compelling vision. Vision answers the question, "What needs to happen next?" Leaders must know the purpose of what they are doing. Purpose answers the question, "Why is it important?" Knowing the answer to this question has guided many leaders through difficult times. Next, leaders must know their mission. God brings people together in community to carry out His will. Mission answers the question, "Who needs to be involved?" Finally, good leaders have clear, concise goals to follow. Typically, a leader will cast the vision, purpose, and mission through four to five goals. Goals answer the question, "How will we do it?"

We have discovered how difficult it is to pick emerging leaders in a group. God will always surprise you with whom He chooses! The most productive approach is to treat every person as if he or she were already a leader. A person may only lead himself or herself, but this is still leading. People become better leaders in direct proportion to our expectations (faith). When we treat people like followers, they become followers. When we treat people like leaders, they become leaders. Jesus chose people from all levels of society to show that good leadership depends on abiding with Him, not the outward signs people often seek. Why do we have a shortage of leaders? Because current leaders refuse to grant new people the opportunity to lead.

Few factors stop a movement of God faster than a lack of godly leadership. Sadly, we have encountered a leadership vacuum in most of the places we have trained people (including America). Godly leaders are the key to shalom – peace, blessing, and righteousness – in a community. One famous quote from Albert Einstein may be paraphrased as follows: "We cannot solve our current problems with our current level of leadership." God is using Follow Jesus Training to equip and motivate many new leaders. We pray the same will happen for you. May the greatest leader of all time fill your heart and mind with every spiritual blessing, make you strong, and increase your influence – the true test of leadership.

TRAINING
CHECKLISTS

One Month before the Training

Enlist a Prayer Team – Enlist a prayer team of twelve people to intercede for the training, before and during the training week. This is VERY important!

Enlist an Apprentice – Enlist an apprentice to team-teach with you, someone who has previously attended *Training Radical Leaders*.

Invite Participants – Invite participants in a culturally sensitive way. Send letters, invitations, or make telephone calls. The best size group for Training Radical Leaders training is a seminar setting of 16-24 leaders. With the help of several apprentices, you can train up to fifty leaders. Training Radical Leaders sessions can also be done effectively weekly with a group of three or more leaders.

Confirm Logistics – Arrange housing, meals, and transportation for leaders as needed.

Secure a Meeting Place – Arrange a meeting room with two tables for supplies in the back of the room, chairs arranged in a circle for participants and plenty of room for learning activities during the sessions. If it is more fitting, arrange for a mat on the floor instead of chairs. Plan to provide two break times every day with coffee, tea, and snacks.

Gather Training Materials – Collect Bibles, a white board or large sheets of paper, student notes, leader notes, color markers or crayons, notebooks (like the ones students use in school), pens or pencils, a Chinlone ball, and prizes.

Arrange Worship Times – Use song sheets or a chorus book for each participant. Find a person in the group who plays guitar and ask him or her to help you lead the worship times.

After the Training

Evaluate Every Part of the Training with Your Apprentice – Spend time reviewing and evaluating the training time with your apprentice. Create a list of positives and negatives. Make plans to improve the training next time you teach it.

Connect with Potential Apprentices about Helping With a Future Training – Contact two or three leaders who have showed leadership potential during the training about helping you with a Training Radical Leaders training in the future.

Encourage Training Participants to Bring a Friend to the Next Training – Challenge training participants to return with ministry partners the next time they attend. Doing so will accelerate the number of leaders who are training other leaders.

F.A.Q.

What should I do if I cannot complete the lesson in an hour and a half?

Remember the process and content are equally important. Following the process builds confidence. Quality content brings education. Both the process and quality content produce transformation. The most common mistake we have noticed in training others is giving too much content and not enough time to practice.

Most *Follow Jesus Training* lessons have a natural break halfway through the lesson. If you find you do not have enough time to complete the lesson, teach the first half of the lesson following the entire training process, and do the rest of the lesson the next time you meet. Depending on the level of education of the people you are training, you may decide to go to this schedule all of time.

Our goal is to help adult learners weave Jesus' leadership style into every part of their life. That takes time and patience, but is well worth the investment.

What does a leadership movement look like?

God is moving in significant ways throughout the nations.

Currently, researchers have documented over eighty people movements. If sharing the gospel drives the "engine" in these movements, then the "wheels" are leadership development. In fact, it is often difficult to say whether they are leadership, discipleship, or church-planting movements. Whatever the name, they all share one quality: men, women, youth, and children in their spheres of influence being like Christ, the greatest leader of all time.

Leadership chains characterize a leadership movement. Small groups of men or women meet for accountability, coaching, and learning. Paul talked about these kinds of chains in 2 Timothy 2:2. A leader receives coaching in one group and gives coaching to another group. Leadership chains continually expand to the sixth or seventh generation in fully developed movements. Any organization, ministry, or people group can only go as far as their leaders can lead them. Therefore, leadership must be intentionally cultivated because leaders are not born. Leaders need to learn how to lead.

In a leadership movement, teenagers learn about the tools of leadership; the vision, purpose, mission, and goals. Men and women in their twenties begin to apply these tools in their business and personal lives. Thirty year olds focus the tools on specific ministries or businesses. When someone is in their forties, he or she begins to see fruit from applying the tools of leadership with perseverance. People in their fifties, who have followed Jesus' leadership style for a long time, serve as models to the younger generations. Usually, people in their sixties can coach many younger men and women as leaders. Saints in their seventies leave a legacy of faithfulness and fruitfulness, even in their old age.

In what ways has the role of a foreign missionary changed over time?

Every mission effort has four phases: discovery, development, deployment, and delegation. Each phase has unique goals and challenges. Each phase also requires a different skill-set from missionaries.

The *discovery* phase includes identifying unreached people, sending pioneer missionaries, and gaining a foothold in an unreached area. The missionary role is to explore, evangelize, and connect with interested nationals. The fruit of this period is a few churches. However, the churches often resemble churches in the sending group's country more than the receiving country and culture. During the discovery phase, missionaries do eighty percent of the work while nationals contribute twenty percent.

The few churches started in the discovery phase continue to grow and start other churches, leading to an association of churches in the *development* phase. Missionaries in this phase help churches network together, evangelize, and begin intentional efforts of discipleship among believers. A small Christian culture begins to take root in the host country. During the development phase, missionaries do sixty percent of the work while nationals contribute forty percent.

The mission moves into the *deployment* phase when several associations of churches form a convention or network. This period typically begins with a hundred groups or churches and continues to pick up momentum. The role of the missionary is to assure continued leadership development, help nationals troubleshoot problem areas, and assist nationals as they implement a strategy to reach their entire people group. During the deployment phase, nationals do sixty percent of the work while missionaries contribute forty percent.

The last phase of every mission is *delegation*. In this phase, missionaries entrust the work to national believers. Missionaries return to the work for times of coaching, celebration, and collaboration. During the delegation phase, nationals do ninety percent of the work while missionaries contribute ten percent. The discovery phase begins again, but this time in the lives and work of the national believers.

Foreign missionaries should recognize that they are currently in the delegation phase in most parts of the world. The main role of a missionary today is coaching, training, and helping national brother and sisters carry out the mission God has given them. One of the goals of Follow Jesus Training is to provide missionaries with simple, reproducible tools for the delegation phase.

What is the "Rule of 5?"

Simply, a person must practice a skill five times before they have the confidence to perform the skill by themselves. After training almost 5,000 people personally in the last nine years, we have seen this principle proven repeatedly.

Training seminars are full of intelligent and capable adults, but most often little change occurs in their lives after the seminar. A typical response to this problem is to make the content more interesting, or more memorable, or (you can fill in the blank). Usually, the problem is not the content, but the fact people have not practiced it enough to make it a part of their life.

Why do you use so many hand motions?

People learn by what they see, what they hear, and what they do. Western educational methods stress the first and second kinds of learning (especially in the lecture format). Many studies document how little learners retain using only speaking and listening. The third learning style – kinesthetic – remains the most neglected approach in training others. We have found hand motions to be the easiest way to teach a group to memorize a large amount of information. Literate and non-literate people alike can retell stories better when combined with action or hand motions.

You should know we did not use hand motions when we started training others with *Follow Jesus Training*. We changed our approach, however, when we altered one of the training goals; we wanted learners to be able to repeat the entire seminar back to us at the end. Memorization is a key ingredient in most Asian learning settings. Now, people can repeat the whole seminar back from memory in the final session because we use hand motions. They could not do so before we started using them. After a few short lessons, learners enjoy the active learning and are amazed they can remember the whole seminar at the end.

After we started using hand motions, we noticed an increase in the number of leaders training leaders. Spiritual training involves more than just the mind. If the heart remains unchanged then no transformation has taken place. Using hand motions helps move what we have learned from the head to the heart. That is why we teach children with hand motions to help them remember important truths for life. Adults, youth, and children can learn in a multi-generational setting when we use hand motions. Personally, I use hand motions regularly in my prayer times to keep me focused on what part of prayer I am focusing on – praise, repent, ask, or yield.

Why are the lessons so simple?

The main reason the lessons are simple is that we follow Jesus's example of teaching in a simple way. He made the complex simple. We make the simple complex. Jesus's concern is life change, not mastering the "newest truth." When we teach in a simple way, children, youth, and adults can learn the lessons in community. You do not need a thousand dollar tracking machine with all the bells and whistles to tell you where "north" is. An inexpensive compass will do.

The book of Proverbs says to seek wisdom above all. Wisdom is the ability to apply knowledge to life skillfully and righteously. We have noticed the more complex a plan is, the more likely it is to fail. Pastors and missionaries throughout the world have strategic mission plans that took weeks or months to develop. Most of those plans sit on a shelf somewhere. Some people argue that the book of Proverbs says to avoid being simple. Proverbs, however, says to avoid being a "simpleton." The wise person does a task in a way others can copy; a simpleton does otherwise.

The good news is that following Jesus does not depend on a person's intellect, talents, schooling, accomplishments, or personality. Following Jesus depends on a person's willingness to obey Jesus' commands immediately, all the time, and from a heart of love. Complex teaching typically creates learners who are not able to apply the lesson to their daily lives. Jesus commands believers to make disciples, teaching them to obey all of His commands. We believe teachers hinder people's obedience when they teach complex lessons which the learner cannot teach to another person.

What are some common mistakes people make when they train others?

Trainers make training mistakes in three areas: people, process, and content. Having trained and been trained by many people, we offer these observations to help you strengthen your skills.

Every learner comes to a training session with previous experiences, knowledge, and skills. Trainers who do not consider this at the beginning of the session run the risk of training learners to do something they already know how to do. A simple question like "What do you already know about this subject?" helps the trainers know the proper level to train. We have seen trainers, however, who assume the learners know more than they know. Untested assumptions always come back to bite you.

Communication solves this problem. People have different learning styles and it is a mistake to base your training on just one or two styles. Doing so guarantees some learners will not benefit like they could with better lesson planning. People also have different needs according to their personality. Training in a way that only appeals to extroverts excludes introverts. Concentrating on people focused on "thinking" are not as effective as lessons that address "feeling" as well.

The training process is another area teachers make mistakes. Training that includes no opportunity for discussion and relies solely on speaking is not training but presenting. Training is a journey that involves the whole person in the mastery of a skill, character quality, or knowledge. We have noticed trainers focus so much on content that they do not give learners the opportunity to talk through what they have learned.

The richest learning times for adults are when they discuss the lesson and its application to their lives. Another common mistake is using the same learning techniques throughout the training time. Any training technique loses effectiveness if used too often. The last mistake is lengthy training sessions. As a rule, we try to teach the lesson one-third of the time. Then, we ask the learners to practice the lesson for one-third of the time. Finally, we lead a discussion about applying the lesson the last one-third of the time. In a ninety minute session, learners usually listen to us speak about twenty minutes.

Typically, the reason training sessions go too long is the trainer is sharing too much content – the final area where trainers make mistakes. Good training content will address knowledge, character, skill, and motivation. If the trainer is from a western background, most likely they will focus on the knowledge part, assuming "knowing" produces the rest. They may speak to character and motivation, but rarely deal with practicing skills.

Most often, trainers train others using the same method modeled to them. Breaking with the past may be necessary, however, for real change to take place in the learner's lives. Excellent training does not strive to present information alone. The goal is transformation. We have noticed trainers who do not adapt their materials to a new setting or culture; they expect rural rice farmers to handle the content as young urban professionals. A lack of prayer is the most common reason for this mistake.

The biggest mistake trainers make, in our experience, is not giving the time learners need to practice what they have learned. Trainers face the temptation to view training as a onetime event and not a continuing journey. A sure sign of an "event outlook" is the attitude, "We have them here. Let's pour as much learning into them as we can." Focusing instead on giving learners a biblical process to train others with takes a paradigm shift. Trainers become more concerned about the person the learner will train, rather than the learner alone. If you find yourself with more content and no practice time, you may be guilty of giving people more than they can reasonably obey or share with others. You set them up for failure, rather than success.

What do you suggest if there are no leaders to train?

Growing leaders attract growing leaders. When you commit to follow Jesus and His leadership style, God will bless and send others to walk with you. We must take the first step of faith, however. Jesus lives in every believer and desires His kingdom to come and His will to be done. Lordship and leadership work together. Remember, we have not because we ask not. Pray for eyes to see the leaders God is developing. Pray for a heart of acceptance and encouragement. Pray for Jesus' perspective on leadership. Fishermen make good apostles.

Concentrate on people God has already given you, not on the people you do not have. Begin to develop people who are following you into stronger leaders. Every person leads someone. Fathers lead their families. Mothers lead their children. Teachers lead their students. Businesspeople lead their communities. The leadership principles taught in *Follow Jesus Training* can be applied in any of these settings. People rise to meet our expectations. Treat each person as if that person is already a leader and watch what God does in his or her life.

Consider hosting a leadership training event. Publicize the meeting through existing leadership groups – the Lion's Club, Chamber of Commerce, village council, or quarter director. Use these training materials to equip business leaders with leadership principles from the greatest leader of all time. Organizing an event will not only give you credibility in the community, but also develop you as a leader. If your people group has no followers of Jesus, train leaders in a "cousin" people group, casting a vision for reaching people who have never heard of Jesus.

What are the first steps for leaders as they begin to train new leaders?

Jesus spent an entire evening in prayer before selecting leaders, so prayer is the best place to start. Pray for leaders to rise from the harvest to lead the harvest. As you pray, remember God looks at the heart and man looks at the outward appearance. Look for faithfulness and character in potential leaders. Too often, we concentrate on talent and first impressions. Spend time in prayer asking God to raise up passionate, spiritual leaders.

After you have prayed, begin consistently sharing a vision of leaders following Jesus' example as a leader. Pray with family and friends, asking God to help you become better leaders together. Ask people that God brings across your path if they would like to learn how to become stronger leaders. Constantly cast the vision of friends helping each other develop into leaders that are more fruitful. As you cast the vision for developing leaders, notice people who are interested and energized by what you say.

The next step is to ask God to show you the leaders He is raising up. Do not try to pick them yourself. Let them "self-select" by their willingness to do the tasks required of leaders. We do not "appoint" leaders, but "anoint" leaders that are already showing themselves faithful. Too often, the very people we would have picked "last" on our list of potential leaders God picked as "first." Look for people dissatisfied with the status quo. Concentrate on people willing to learn and follow. Do not be disappointed if leadership at the top tier of an organization shows little interest.

Finally, start to take steps in fulfilling your own Jesus Plan. Nothing attracts present and potential leaders like action. People like to be a part of a winning team. As God blesses your Jesus Plan, He will also send people to help you. Most often God will send family members, friends, and successful business people. Leaders have followers. When you follow Jesus, it will give others a clear direction they can also follow. Someone has to start the journey among your people group. Let it be you!

What are different settings that trainers have used *Training Radical Leaders*?

If you only have one day, we recommend teaching the "How did Jesus Train Leaders," "Seven Qualities of a Great Leader," and "Eight Roles of Christ" lessons. This will equip leaders with the skills, character, and passion to train other leaders. When they ask you to return, teach the rest of the lessons to fill in their leadership knowledge and competency, and give them a good strategic plan to follow. This approach works best in settings where people are busy and have little time to attend training sessions.

If you can only meet weekly or every two weeks, we recommend teaching the seminar lesson-by-lesson. The skills build upon each other and leaders will gain a solid foundation by the end of 10 or 20 weeks. Encourage leaders to train new leaders between meetings with the lessons you are giving them. This approach works best when people are busy but able to commit a specific time to study each week. Ask leaders to reteach outside class any lesson others miss because of illness or unforeseen circumstance.

If you have three days, we recommend following the order in this manual. Allow plenty of discussion and use break times for one-on-one meetings with leaders. At the end of each session, ask leaders to respond to the following question: "What is God saying to you about this lesson?" Allow them to process their answers with the group. Adults learn best when discussing and wrestling with issues together. You will also gain insight about needs of the group. This approach works best in Seminary or Bible School settings, with full-time ministers, and in rural or village settings where people work according to farming seasons.

PART II

LEADERSHIP TRAINING

1

WELCOME

Trainers and leaders introduce each other in the first lesson. Leaders then learn the difference between the Greek method and the Hebrew method of training. Jesus used both methods and we should do the same. The Hebrew method is the most helpful for training leaders and the one most often used in *Training Radical Leaders*.

The lesson goal is for leaders to understand Jesus' strategy to reach the world. The five parts of Jesus' strategy include: Be Strong in God, Share the Gospel, Make Disciples, Start Groups that Become Churches, and Train Leaders. Leaders review the lessons in *Follow Jesus Training, Part 1: Making Radical Disciples* that equip believers to succeed in each part of Jesus' strategy. Leaders also practice casting a vision of following Jesus' strategy for others. The session finishes with a charge to follow Jesus and obey His commands every day.

PRAISE

Sing two choruses or hymns together.

Ask a respected leader to pray for God's presence and blessing during the training seminar.

BEGINNING

Introducing the Trainers

Trainers and leaders sit in a circle to begin the opening session. To promote an informal atmosphere, remove any tables set up earlier.

Trainers model how leaders will introduce themselves.

The trainer and apprentice introduce each other. They share the other person's name, information about their family, ethnic group (if fitting), and a way that God has blessed the group they are leading during the previous month.

Introducing the Leaders

Divide leaders into pairs.

"Introduce your partner in the same way that my apprentice and I did."

Leaders should learn their partner's name, information about their family, ethnic group (if fitting), and one way that God has blessed the group they are leading the previous month. Encourage them to write the information in their student notebook so they do not forget it when they introduce their partner.

After about five minutes, ask leader pairs to introduce themselves to at least five other partners in the same way that you introduced your partner to them.

How Did Jesus Train Leaders?

Ask leaders to place their chairs in rows – the traditional method of teaching. They should form at least two rows and an aisle down the middle. Leaders sit in the rows, while the trainers stand at the front.

"We call this the 'Greek' method of teaching. The teacher shares knowledge, students ask a few questions, and everyone addresses the teacher first. Typically, teachers organize their class this way, especially with children."

Ask leaders to place their chairs back in a circle like the one at the beginning of the session. Leaders and trainers form a circle sitting together.

"We call this the 'Hebrew' method of teaching. The teacher asks a few questions, students discuss the subject, and everyone addresses the one who is speaking, not the teacher alone. Teachers sometimes use this method when teaching adults. Which method of teaching did Jesus use?"

Allow students to discuss the question and then say "Both." Jesus used the Greek method when he addressed the crowds and the Hebrew method when he was training the disciples as leaders.

"Which method do most teachers in your setting use?"

Teachers use the Greek method more often. As a result, we feel most comfortable in that setting.

"In these training sessions, we will show how to train leaders the way Jesus did. Most of the sessions in Training Radical Leaders will use the 'Hebrew' method, because Jesus used that method when he trained leaders. We want to imitate Him."

PLAN

"Our goal in this lesson is to understand Jesus' strategy to reach the world, so we can follow him."

Who Builds the Church?

> – Matthew 16:18 – Now I say to you that you are Peter (which means 'rock'), and upon this rock I will build my church, and all the powers of hell will not conquer it. (NLT)

"Jesus is the one who builds His church."

Why is it Important Who Builds the Church?

> – Psalm 127:1 – Unless the LORD builds a house, its builders labor over it in vain; unless the LORD watches over a city, the watchman stays alert in vain. (HCSB)

"Unless Jesus builds the church, our work will come to nothing. During his earthly ministry and throughout church history, Jesus has always built his church using the same strategy. Let's learn His strategy so we can follow Him."

How Does Jesus Build His Church?

Draw the diagram below, section by section, while you share Jesus' strategy to reach the world.

Be Strong in God

> – Luke 2:52 – Jesus became wise, and he grew strong. God was pleased with him and so were the people. (CEV)

> – Luke 4:14 – (after His temptation) And Jesus returned to Galilee in the power of the Spirit, and news about Him spread through all the surrounding district. (NASB)

"The first tactic in Jesus' strategy is 'Be Strong in God.' Spiritual leadership depends on a clean and close relationship with God. For us to be strong, we must abide in Jesus.

Be Strong in God – Hold arms up and pose like a strong man.

As we abide in Jesus, we pray, obey His commands, walk in the Spirit, and join Jesus where he is working."

REVIEW the "Pray," "Obey," and "Walk" lessons with hand motions in *Follow Jesus Training, Part 1: Making Radical Disciples*:

"These lessons train us how to abide in Christ. They help us to train others to abide in Him, too. Part of being strong in the Lord is obeying His commands. The rest of Jesus' strategy consists of commands we should obey immediately, all the time, and from a heart of love."

Share the Gospel

> – Mark 1:14, 15 – Later on, after John was arrested, Jesus went into Galilee, where he preached God's Good News. "The time promised by God has come at last!" he announced. "The Kingdom of God is near! Repent of your sins and believe the Good News!" (NLT)

"We grow strong in God by praying and walking in the Spirit. Another way we grow strong in God is obeying Jesus' commands. Jesus commands us to join Him where He is working and share the good news."

Share the Gospel – Make a throwing motion with your right hand like you are casting seeds.

"For most people, sharing a testimony about how God has saved them is a good starting place when sharing the good news with others. People listen with interest and enjoy hearing our story. Sharing our testimony also allows us to see if the Holy Spirit is working, so we can join him.

When we see where God is working, we share the simple gospel. Make sure to plant the gospel seed. Remember: no seed, no harvest!"

REVIEW the "Go," "Share," and "Sow" lessons with hand motions in *Follow Jesus Training, Part 1: Making Radical Disciples.*

"Don't fall for one of Satan's traps at this point. Many believers mistakenly think they need to be stronger in God before they share the gospel. They do not realize the opposite is true. We grow stronger after we have obeyed Jesus commands, not before. Obey Jesus' commands by sharing the gospel and then you will grow stronger in your faith. If you wait until you feel "strong enough," you will never share your faith."

Make Disciples

> – Matthew 4:19 – *"Come, follow me," Jesus said, "and I will make you fishers of men."*

"As we abide in Jesus and obey His command to share the gospel, people will respond and want to grow as believers."

> *Make Disciples – Hands on heart and then lifted in worship. Hands on waist, then lifted in classic prayer pose. Hands point toward mind, then, lowered to look like you are reading a book. Hold arms up like a strong man pose, and then make a sweeping motion as if you are casting seed.*

"The most important command to obey is to love God and love people. We show the new followers of Jesus how to do that in practical ways. We also teach them how to pray, obey

Jesus' commands, walk in the Spirit, go where Jesus is working, share their testimony, and share the simple gospel, so they can be strong in God, too."

REVIEW the "Love" lesson with hand motions in Follow Jesus Training, Part 1: Making Radical Disciples.

Start Groups and Churches

> *– Matthew 16:18 – I also say to you that you are Peter, and upon this rock I will build My church; and the gates of Hades will not overpower it.*

"As we abide in Jesus and obey His commands, we share the gospel and make disciples. Then, we follow Jesus' example and start groups that worship, pray, study, and minister together. Jesus is starting these kinds of groups all over the world to strengthen His church and help churches start new churches for His glory."

> *Start Groups and Churches – Hands make a "gathering in" motion, like you are asking people to gather around you.*

Develop Leaders

> *– Matthew 10:5-8 – These twelve Jesus sent out with the following instructions: "Do not go among the Gentiles or enter any town of the Samaritans. Go rather to the lost sheep of Israel. As you go, preach this message: 'The kingdom of heaven is near.' Heal the sick, raise the dead, cleanse those who have leprosy, drive out demons. Freely you have received, freely give.*

"As we abide in Christ, we show our love for Him by obeying His commands. We share the gospel so lost people can come back to the family of God. We make disciples who love both

God and people. We start groups that worship, pray, study, and minister together. More groups create a need for more leaders. Following the 222 Principle in 2 Timothy 2:2, we train leaders, who train leaders, who train even more leaders."

Develop Leaders – Stand at attention and salute like a soldier.

REVIEW the "Multiply" lesson with hand motions in Follow Jesus Training, Part 1: Making Radical Disciples.

"Please avoid a common misunderstanding of Jesus' strategy. Many believers try to follow these commands sequentially. First, they think, we will evangelize; then, we will make disciples, and so on. Jesus, however, showed us to obey all the commands in every setting. For example, as we share the gospel, we are already training the person how to be a follower of Jesus. As we make disciples, we help the new believers find an existing group or start a new one. From the start, we display the habits of a passionate, spiritual leader.

This five-part strategy describes how Jesus builds His church. The disciples imitated Jesus' strategy in the early church. Paul copied this strategy in his mission to the Gentiles. Successful spiritual leaders throughout church history have done the same. When leaders have joined Jesus in His strategy to reach the world, God has blessed entire countries in significant ways. May we follow Jesus' strategy and see God's glory come in this country!"

Memory Verse

– I Corinthians 11:1 – Be imitators of me, just as I also am of Christ. (NASB)

Everyone stands and says the memory verse ten times together. The first six times, they may use their Bible or student notes. The last four times, they say the verse from memory. Say the verse reference before quoting the verse each time and sit down when finished.

Following this routine will help the trainers know which teams have finished the lesson in the "Practice" section.

PRACTICE

"Now, let's practice what we have learned about Jesus' strategy to reach the world. We will take turns sharing the strategy with each other. Then, we will have the confidence to teach others."

Ask leaders to divide into pairs.

"Take a sheet of paper. Fold the paper in half. Now, fold it in half again just as I am showing you. This gives you four panels to draw the picture of Jesus' strategy on when you unfold the paper."

Ask leaders to practice drawing the picture of Jesus' strategy and explaining it to each other. *Both leaders* draw the strategy picture *at the same time.* Only one person shares the explanation, though. Leaders do not need to review the lessons from *Making Radical Disciples* as they are drawing the picture.

When the first person in the pair finishes drawing and explaining the picture of Jesus' strategy, the second person does the same. *Both partners* draw a new picture *the second time.* Partners should then *stand* and say the memory verse together ten times, following the pattern you taught earlier.

"When you finish drawing the picture two times and saying the memory verse ten times with your first partner, find another partner and practice this lesson with them in the same way.

When you finish practicing with your second partner, find another partner."

"Do this until you have practiced drawing and explaining Jesus' strategy to reach the world with four different people."

(When leaders finish this activity, they should have filled out the front and back of their paper, with eight pictures of Jesus' strategy in all.)

ENDING

JESUS SAYS "FOLLOW ME"

> – Matthew 9:9 – As Jesus went on from there, he saw a man named Matthew sitting at the tax collector's booth. "Follow me," he told him, and Matthew got up and followed him.

"Tax collectors were some of the most despised people in the time of Jesus. No one would have believed Jesus would call Matthew because he was a tax collector.

The fact Jesus called Matthew shows us he cares more about the present than the past. You may think that God cannot work in your life because you have committed too many sins. You may feel ashamed of remarks you have made in the past. The good news, though, is that God uses anyone who chooses to follow Jesus today. God is looking for people who are willing to abide and obey.

When we follow someone, we copy him or her. An apprentice copies his master to learn a trade. Students become like their teachers. All of us copy someone. The person we copy is the person we become.

The purpose of Follow Jesus Training is to show leaders how to copy Jesus. We believe the more we copy Him the more we will be like Him. So in this training, we will ask leadership questions, study the Bible, discover how Jesus led others, and practice following Him."

Ask a respected leader in the group to close the lesson with a prayer of blessing and dedication to follow Jesus' strategy to reach the world.

2

TRAIN LIKE
JESUS

A common problem in growing churches or groups is the need for more leaders. Efforts to train leaders often fall short because we do not have a simple process to follow. The goal of this lesson is to explain how Jesus trained leaders, so we can imitate Him.

Jesus trained leaders by asking them about the progress made in their mission and discussing any problems the leaders had faced. He also prayed for them and helped them make plans to further the mission. An important part of their training was practicing the skills they would need in their future ministries.

In Lesson 2, leaders apply this leadership training process to their group as well as Jesus' strategy to reach the world.

Finally, leaders develop a "Training Tree" that helps coordinate training and prayer for the leaders they are training.

PRAISE

Sing two worship songs together. Ask a leader to pray for this session.

PROGRESS

Ask another leader in the training to share a short testimony (three minutes) of how God is blessing his or her group. After the leader shares a testimony, ask the group to pray for him or her.

PROBLEM

"Churches and groups recognize they need more leaders, but many times do not know how to train new ones. Current leaders take on more responsibility and jobs until they burn out. Followers ask leaders to do more and more with less and less until the leaders finally give up. Churches and groups in every culture and country face this problem regularly."

PLAN

"We can learn to train passionate, spiritual leaders. The goal of this lesson is to show how Jesus trained leaders, so we can copy Him."

How Did Jesus Train Leaders?

– Luke 10:17 – When the seventy-two disciples returned, they

joyfully reported to him, "Lord, even the demons obey us when
we use your name!" (NLT)

Progress

"The disciples returned from their mission and reported the progress they had made to Jesus. In the same way, we talk with leaders we are training. We show a personal interest in how their family is doing and progress made in their ministry."

Progress – Roll hands over each other moving upwards.

— — — — —

– Matthew 17:19 – Afterward the disciples asked Jesus privately, "Why couldn't we cast out that demon?" (NLT)

Problems

"The disciples met problems during their ministry and asked Jesus to help them understand why they had failed. In the same way, we ask leaders to share the problems they are facing so we can seek God together for solutions."

Problems – Place hands on each side of your head and pretend to pull hair.

— — — — —

– Luke 10:1 – After this the Lord appointed seventy-two others
and sent them two by two ahead of him to every town and place
where he was about to go.

Plans

"Jesus gave the disciples simple, spiritual, and strategic plans to follow in their mission. In the same way, we help leaders make a plan for their 'next tactic' that is simple, dependent on God, and addresses the problems they face."

> *Plans – Spread out your left hand like paper and "write" on it with the right hand.*

— — — — —

> *– John 4:1-2 – Jesus knew the Pharisees had heard that he was baptizing and making more disciples than John (though Jesus himself did not baptize them—his disciples did). (NLT)*

Practice

"The discovery that the disciples, not Jesus, baptized new believers surprises many leaders. In several instances like this one, Jesus allowed the disciples to practice the tasks that they would perform after He returned to heaven. In the same way, we give leaders an opportunity to practice the skills they will need when they return to their ministries. We give them a 'safe place' to practice, make mistakes, and gain confidence."

> *Practice – Move arms up and down as if you are lifting weights.*

— — — — —

> *– Luke 22:31-32 – Jesus said, "Simon, listen to me! Satan has demanded the right to test each one of you, as a farmer does when he separates wheat from the husks. But Simon, I have prayed that your faith will be strong. And when you have come back to me, help the others." (CEV)*

Prayer

"Jesus already knew that Peter would make mistakes and face the temptation to quit. Jesus also knew that prayer is key to power and perseverance in our walk with God. Praying for those that we are leading is the most important support we can give them."

Prayer – Make classic "praying hands" pose close to your face.

Memory Verse

– Luke 6:40 – A disciple is not above his teacher, but everyone who is fully trained will be like his teacher. (HCSB)

Everyone stands and says the memory verse ten times together. The first six times, they may use their Bible or student notes. The last four times, they say the verse from memory. Everyone should say the verse reference before quoting the verse each time. Ask leaders to sit down when they finish.

Following this routine will help the trainers know which teams have finished the lesson in the "Practice" section.

PRACTICE

Divide leaders into groups of four.

Walk leaders through the training process step-by-step, giving them 7-8 minutes to discuss each of the following sections.

Review

"What are the five parts in Jesus' strategy to reach the world?"

Draw the diagram on a white board as leaders answer.

Progress

"Which part of Jesus' strategy to reach the world is easiest for your group to carry out?"

Problems

"Share problems your group has faced following Jesus' strategy to reach the world. Which part of Jesus' strategy is the hardest for your group to carry out?"

Plans

"Share one task you will lead your group to do in the next 30 days that will help them follow Jesus' strategy to reach the world more effectively."

Everyone should record their partners' plans so they can pray for them later.

Practice

"Share one skill that you personally will practice in the next 30 days to help you improve as a leader in your group."

Everyone records their partners' practice item so they can pray for them later.

After each person has shared the skill they will practice, group members stand and say the memory verse ten times together.

Prayer

"In your small group, spend time praying for each other's plans and the skill you will practice the next 30 days to improve as a leader."

ENDING

Training Tree

"The 'Training Tree' is a helpful tool to organize and pray for the people we are training to be leaders."

On a white board, draw the trunk of a tree, the roots of the tree, and a line showing the grass level.

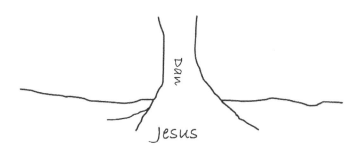

"I start drawing my Training Tree like this. Draw a trunk, then some roots, and finally the grass. The Bible says that we are rooted in Christ, so I will put His name here. Since this drawing is my Training Tree, I put my name on the trunk."

Label the area under the roots "Jesus" and write your name on the trunk of the tree.

"Jesus invested most of his leadership training with three people: Peter, James, and John. I want to imitate Him, so I will do the same. God has given me three leaders to invest most of my training time in."

Draw three lines upward and outward from the trunk of the tree. At the top of each line, put the name of the three main leaders you are training.

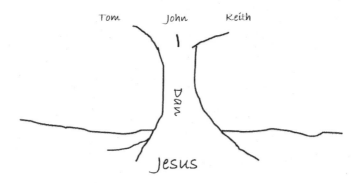

"Jesus trained three and showed them how to train others. If each one trained three others (like Jesus), that gives us twelve all together. Hmmm. Jesus had twelve disciples. Isn't that interesting?"

Draw three lines upward and outward from each of the three main leaders you are training. Label the top of each line with the name of a person your main leaders are training. Share any stories the Holy Spirit brings to mind about your Training Tree. Draw leaves around the limbs to complete your tree.

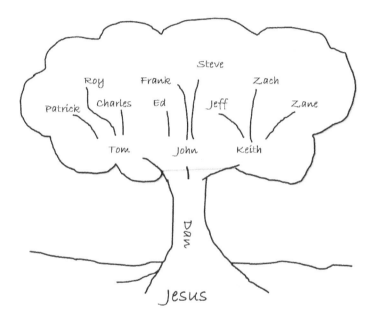

"Now I would like you to draw your own 'Training Tree.' You may need to write some of the names 'in faith' but do your best to have twelve people on the Training Tree. The first three branches are the main leaders you will train. Each of those leaders has three branches containing the leaders they spend most of their time training."

While leaders are drawing their "Training Trees," share the following:

"I am often asked, 'How should I train leaders?' Jesus said to ask and you will receive. Have you asked him for what you need? This training will give you the tools you need to train leaders.

Others say, 'I don't know anyone I can train as a leader.' Jesus said to seek and you will find. Have you been seeking people to train or waiting for them to come to you? He said 'seek' not 'wait.'

Still others ask, 'Where should I start training leaders?' Jesus said to knock and the door will open for you. Have you been knocking? God will bless us with direction when we take the first step of faith.

Most often, the reason we do not have a "Training Tree" is we have not asked, knocked, or sought one. When we obey Jesus' commands, from a heart of love, God will give us more training opportunities than we can imagine.

This tool will help you coach other leaders in progress, problems, plans, practice, and prayer."

Ask a leader in the group to close the session in prayer.

"Pray for the leaders on our Training Trees and the plans we have made in our small groups. Pray for the items we are going to practice and improve as a leader during the next month."

3

LEAD LIKE JESUS

Jesus Christ is the greatest leader of all time. No person has influenced more people more often than He has. Lesson 3 introduces the seven qualities of a great leader, based on Jesus' leadership style. Leaders then reflect on the strengths and weaknesses of their own leadership experiences. A team-building game ends the session teaching the power of "shared leadership."

Everything rises and falls on the heart of the leader, so we look at how Jesus led the disciples, so we can imitate Him. Jesus loved them to the end, understood His mission, knew the problems in the group, gave His followers an example to follow, confronted with kindness, and knew God was blessing His obedience. Everything flows from our heart. Therefore, the attitude of our heart is where we must begin as leaders.

PRAISE

Sing two worship songs together. Ask a leader to pray for this session.

PROGRESS

Ask another leader in the training to share a short testimony (three minutes) of how God is blessing his or her group. After the leader shares a testimony, ask the group to pray for him or her.

Alternatively, model a coaching time with a leader using the "Progress, Problems, Plan, Practice, Prayer" leadership training process.

PROBLEM

"The world is full of leaders with different leadership styles. As a follower of Jesus, what should my leadership style look like?"

PLAN

"Jesus is the greatest leader of all time. No person has influenced more people more often than He has. In this lesson, we will look at how Jesus led others, so we can imitate Him."

Who Did Jesus Say Is the Greatest Leader?

> – Matthew 20:25-28 – But Jesus called them together and said, "You know that the rulers in this world lord it over their people, and officials flaunt their authority over those under them. But among you it will be different. Whoever wants to be a leader among you must be your servant, and whoever wants to be first

among you must become your slave. For even the Son of Man came not to be served but to serve others and to give his life as a ransom for many." (NLT)

"The greatest leader is the greatest servant."

Salute like a solider and then put hands together and bow like a servant.

What are Seven Qualities of a Great Leader?

– John 13:1-17 – [1]*It was just before the Passover Feast. Jesus knew that the time had come for him to leave this world and go to the Father. Having loved his own who were in the world, he now showed them the full extent of his love.*

[2]*The evening meal was being served, and the devil had already prompted Judas Iscariot, son of Simon, to betray Jesus.*

[3]*Jesus knew that the Father had put all things under his power, and that he had come from God and was returning to God*

[4]*so he got up from the meal, took off his outer clothing, and wrapped a towel around his waist.*

[5]*After that, he poured water into a basin and began to wash his disciples' feet, drying them with the towel that was wrapped around him.*

[6]*He came to Simon Peter, who said to him, "Lord, are you going to wash my feet?"*

[7]*Jesus replied, "You do not realize now what I am doing, but later you will understand."*

[8]*"No," said Peter, "you shall never wash my feet." Jesus answered, "Unless I wash you, you have no part with me."*

[9]*"Then, Lord," Simon Peter replied, "not just my feet but my hands and my head as well!"*

[10]*Jesus answered, "A person who has had a bath needs only to wash his feet; his whole body is clean. And you are clean, though not every one of you."*

[11]*For he knew who was going to betray him, and that was why he said not everyone was clean.*

[12]*When he had finished washing their feet, he put on his clothes and returned to his place. "Do you understand what I have done for you?" he asked them.*

[13]*"You call me 'Teacher' and 'Lord,' and rightly so, for that is what I am.*

[14]*Now that I, your Lord and Teacher, have washed your feet, you also should wash one another's feet.*

[15]*I have set you an example that you should do as I have done for you.*

[16]*I tell you the truth, no servant is greater than his master, nor is a messenger greater than the one who sent him.* [17]*Now that you know these things, you will be blessed if you do them.*

1. Great Leaders Love People

"In verse 1, Jesus and the disciples were sharing the last supper before Jesus was crucified. The Bible says that Jesus loved them to the end and showed them how much He loved them at this supper.

As a leader, people can be hard to love when they make mistakes, but Jesus loved the people He led until the end.

As a leader, people can be hard to love when they criticize you, but Jesus loved the people He led until the end.

As a leader, people can be hard to love when they let you down, but Jesus loved the people He led until the end."

Love people – Pat chest with hand.

2. Great Leaders Know Their Mission

"In verse 3, the Bible says that Jesus knew where He had come from, where He was going, and that God had put everything under His power.

Jesus knew He had come to the earth for a purpose.

Jesus knew He had come to the earth to die on the cross for our sins.

Jesus knew He had come to earth to defeat Satan and restore us to God.

God gives each person a unique mission to fulfill while on earth. Great leaders know their mission and inspire others to follow them."

Know their mission – Salute as if a soldier and shake head, "yes."

3. Great Leaders serve their followers

"In verse 4, Jesus got up from the meal and took off his outer garments. Then, he wrapped a towel around his waist and began to wash the disciples' feet.

Leaders of the world expect their followers to serve them. Leaders like Jesus, however, serve their followers.

Leaders of the world exert control and power over those they lead. Leaders like Jesus, though, empower those that follow them."

"Worldly leaders focus on themselves and not the people they lead. In contrast, leaders like Jesus focus on the needs of their followers, knowing God will meet their own needs as they care for others. God blesses us so we can bless others."

Serve Their Followers – Bow with both hands in classic prayer position.

4. Great Leaders correct with kindness

"In verses 6 through 9, Peter made several mistakes, but each time Jesus corrected him with kindness.

Peter told Jesus not to wash his feet. Jesus told him it was necessary for their friendship. He corrected him with kindness.

Peter then told Jesus to wash his whole body. Jesus told him that he was already clean, again correcting him with kindness.

Leaders of the world criticize, blame, and push people down. Leaders like Jesus correct with kindness, encourage their followers, and pull people up."

Correct with Kindness – Make a heart sign with index fingers and thumbs of both hands.

5. Great Leaders know current problems in the group

"In verses 10 and 11, the Bible tells us that Jesus knew Judas was a problem in the group and would betray Him.

Understanding where the problems in a group exist and facing them is an important part of leadership. Many leaders try to hide from problems confronting their group, but the problems only get larger.

Notice how Jesus showed restraint in his dealings with Judas, knowing that God is the one who repays evil deeds, not leaders themselves."

> *Problems in the group – Place hands on sides of head as if you have a headache.*

6. Great Leaders give a good example to follow

"In verses 12 through 16, Jesus explained why He had washed the disciple's feet. He was their leader, yet He washed their feet, the task of a servant. Jesus showed the disciples that leadership includes serving one another.

Followers reflect and imitate their leaders. If we are following Jesus, those who follow us as leaders are following Jesus, as well."

> *Give a good example – Point toward heaven and shake head "yes."*

7. Great Leaders know they are blessed

"In verse 17, Jesus told the disciples God would bless them as they led others by serving them.

Leading others is difficult at times, but those who follow Jesus know they are blessed.

Leading others is lonely at times, but Jesus blesses those who lead with His presence.

Followers do not always appreciate their leaders, but Jesus promises God's support when we follow His example of leading by serving others."

Know they are blessed – Lift hands in praise to heaven.

Memory Verse

– John 13:14-15 – Now that I, your Lord and Teacher, have washed your feet, you also should wash one another's feet. I have set you an example that you should do as I have done for you.

Everyone stands and says the memory verse ten times together. The first six times, they may use their Bible or student notes. The last four times, they say the verse from memory. Say the verse reference before quoting the verse each time and sit down when finished.

Following this routine will help the trainers know which teams have finished the lesson in the "Practice" section.

PRACTICE

Divide leaders into groups of four.

"Now, we are going to use the same training process Jesus used to practice what we have learned in this leadership lesson."

Walk leaders through the training process step-by-step, giving them 7-8 minutes to discuss each of the following sections.

Progress

"Share with your group which of the seven qualities of a great leader is the easiest for you."

Problems

"Share with your group which of the seven qualities of a great leader is most challenging for you."

Plans

"Share one task you will lead your group to do in the next 30 days that will help them follow Jesus' example of leadership."

Everyone should record their partners' plans so they can pray for them later.

Practice

"Share one skill that you personally will practice in the next 30 days to help you improve as a leader in your group."

Everyone records their partners' practice item so they can pray for them later.

After each person has shared the skill they will practice, group members stand and say the memory verse ten times together.

Prayer

"Spend time praying for each other's plans and the skill you will practice the next 30 days to improve as a leader."

ENDING

Chinlone

Ask six volunteers to display their Chinlone* ability to the group. Help the six make a playing circle in the middle of the room.

"I have arranged for a famous Chinlone team to show their skills. Let's clap our hands to show appreciation for them coming."

Arrange players with one person at the front of the group as the "leader." Ask the others to make two rows facing the leader.

"First, our famous Chinlone team is going to show how to play Chinlone the 'Greek' way. Listen to the rules they will follow. Each person must kick the Chinlone ball to the leader. After the leader receives the ball, he will kick the ball to another player. We will penalize players who kick the ball to other players, rather than to the leader."

Ask the team to show the "Greek" way to play Chinlone. Playing Chinlone this way will be awkward and confusing for the players. In a humorous way, grab people who hit the ball to someone other than the leader. Shout, "Penalty!" Correct their mistake and show them that they should kick the ball only to the leader.

"What happened when they played Chinlone this way?" (Playing the game with these rules was difficult. The players looked bored. It was not fun)

Now, ask the players to form a regular Chinlone circle, but put the "leader" in the middle.

"This time we will have the Chinlone group perform using the Hebrew way, but with a leader who tries to control everything. We will use the same rules as before – players must kick the ball to the leader who then kicks it to others."

The team will perform better this time, but the leader will show signs of fatigue after a few minutes of play. Call any penalties in a humorous way if players kick the ball to someone other than the leader.

"What happened when they played Chinlone this way?" (The leader worked hard and got very tired. The players made many mistakes. It was boring.)

Have players form a traditional Chinlone circle with every person, including the leader, in the circle. Tell them they do not have to kick the ball to the leader each time. Ask them to play Chinlone the way they always do.

"Now, we will have the famous Chinlone team show how to play Chinlone the true Hebrew way."

Let them play for several minutes until everyone in the seminar is enjoying watching them and making comments about their play.

"What happened when they played Chinlone this way?

(The whole team joined in. The whole team was successful. They made some amazing plays.)

The third way of playing Chinlone is a good example of servant leadership. The leader is helping everyone in the group take part and contribute. The leader does not manage everything, but give others freedom to express their unique style. This is the example of leadership that Jesus gave us to follow."

Ask a leader in the group to close the session in prayer.

"Pray for all of us as leaders to lead like Jesus and for the plans we have made in our small groups. Pray also for the skills we will practice to improve as a leader during the next 30 days."

*Chinlone is the name of a game typically played by males in Myanmar. Participants make a circle and pass a cane ball to each other using only their feet. The goal of Chinlone is to keep the ball from falling to the ground for as long as possible. Players often perfect special kicks and moves to impress others. Height and accuracy of the pass bring the most applause from onlookers and participants.

People play Chinlone throughout Asia, but each country has a different name for the game. Check with local residents to find out the name of the game in the area where you are training.

If you are training leaders in an area that does not have a game like "Chinlone," you may substitute a hacky sack for the ball. Use a balloon to carry out the same training point.

4

GROW STRONG

The leaders you train are leading groups and learning how demanding leading others can be. Leaders face significant spiritual warfare from outside their group and personality differences within the group. A key to effective leadership is identifying different personality types and learning how to work effectively with them as a team. The "Grow Strong" lesson gives leaders a simple way to help people discover their personality type. When we understand how God has made us, we have strong clues about how we can grow stronger in Him.

There are eight personality types: soldier, seeker, shepherd, sower, son/daughter, saint, servant, and steward. After helping leaders discover their type, trainers discuss strengths and weaknesses of each type. Many people assume God loves the personality type their cultures values most. Other leaders believe that leadership ability depends on personality. These limiting beliefs are simply not true. The session ends stressing leaders should treat people as individuals. Leadership training must address individual needs and not be one-size-fits-all.

PRAISE

Sing two worship songs together. Ask a leader to pray for this session.

PROGRESS

Ask another leader in the training to share a short testimony (three minutes) of how God is blessing his or her group. After the leader shares a testimony, ask the group to pray for him or her.

Alternatively, model a coaching time with a leader using the "Progress, Problems, Plan, Practice, Prayer" leadership training model.

PROBLEM

"Leaders often mistakenly expect their followers to act and react the same way. God, however, has created people with many different personalities. One key to effective leadership is recognizing different personality types and learning how to work most effectively with them as a team.

Jesus is a son and wants love and unity to abound in his family. Understanding different personalities will help us love others more."

PLAN

"In this lesson, we will learn eight different personality types. You will discover which personality type God has given you, and how to help others recognize their own personality type. Every believer can grow stronger in the Lord when they understand how God has made them."

Which Personality Has God Given You?

Ask leaders to draw a big circle on a clean sheet of paper in their notebooks.

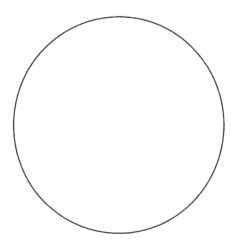

"The circle I am drawing represents all the people in the world."

Ask leaders to draw a horizontal line that bisects the circle in half. Label the right side of the circle "relationships" and label the left side of the circle "tasks."

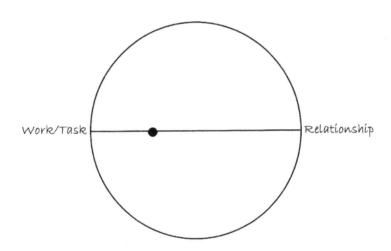

"Every person falls into one of two groups: people who are more 'task-focused' and people who are more 'relationship' focused. God created both types of people, so neither one is better or worse; this is just the way God has made people. Choose a point on the line that you think best represents the kind of person you are."

(A more task-centered person will put a dot on the line closer to the left side. A more relationship-centered person will put a dot on the line closer to the right side. If the person is half relationship and half task, tell them to put their mark close to the middle line, but on one side or the other.)

"Share your results with a neighbor and see if your neighbor agrees with the point you chose. Take about five minutes to do this."

Ask leaders to draw a vertical line that cuts the circle into four equal parts. Label the top of the circle "extrovert" and the bottom of the circle "introvert."

"Everyone in the world also fall into two more groups: those who are more 'outward' oriented (extroverts) and those that are more 'inward' oriented (introverts). Neither focus is better or worse than the other one. This is just the way God makes people.

Choose the place on the vertical line that best represents your preference."

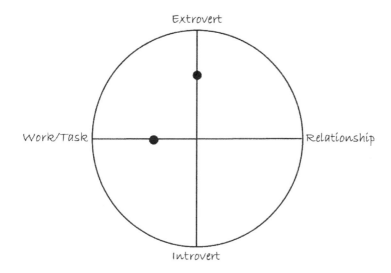

(An outward person would mark closer to the top of the circle. An inward person would make a mark toward the bottom of the circle. If the person is half extrovert and half introvert, tell them to put their mark close to the middle line, but on one side or the other.)

"Share your results with a neighbor and see if your neighbor agrees with the point you chose. Take about three minutes to do this."

Ask leaders to draw two diagonal lines (an "X") which will now give the circle eight equal pieces.

Leaders then draw a dotted-line box to determine which piece their personality falls.

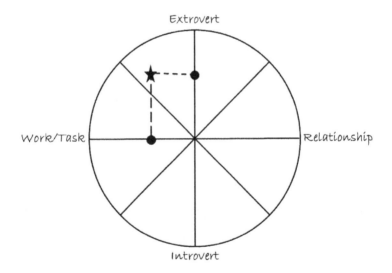

The illustration below shows the completed diagram of a person with a seeker personality.

Starting at the 9:00-10:30 slice, go clockwise and explain the following eight kinds of personalities:

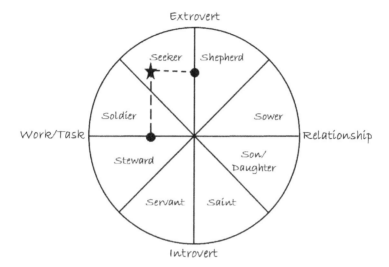

Write the name of the personality type in the blank as you explain their positive and negative qualities.

Soldier

High task, a little more outward than inward.

Positive: Sees what is necessary for victory, determined and honorable, "whatever it takes" attitude.

Negative: May be dominating and insensitive, may win the battle but lose the war.

Seeker

High outward, a little more task than relationship.

Positive: Sees new opportunities, networks well, is an entrepreneur.

Negative: May seek pleasure, may be unable to focus on one task, may think that new is always better.

Shepherd

High outward, a little more relationship than task.

Positive: Sees the spiritual needs of people, enjoys leading groups, and excels at encouraging people in their emotional struggles.

Negative: May be bossy, may start cliques, may struggle to cooperate with existing leadership.

Sower

High relationship, a little more outward than inward.

Positive: Sees potential in people, coaches, constantly improving self.

Negative: May sow strife, struggles with discouragement, talks about favorite subjects too often.

Son or Daughter

High relationship, a little more inward than outward.

Positive: Sees what it takes for others to feel "a part of the family," keeps the peace, and stresses the importance of the individual.

Negative: May believe their family is "best," may be jealous and insecure.

Saint

High inward, a little more relationship than task.

Positive: Sees ways people can connect with God, upholds traditions, is the moral voice of the community.

Negative: May appear "holier than thou," struggles with accepting others, sometimes legalistic.

Servant

High inward, a little more task than relationship.

Positive: Sees how to meet the physical needs of people, loyal, works best behind the scenes.

Negative: Serves others but may not take care of their own family, accepts change slowly, has difficulty seeing the big picture.

Steward

High task, a little more inward than outward.

Positive: Sees the best way to organize resources, is wise and practical.

Negative: May bog down in bureaucracy, lack empathy, or place needs of the organization over the real needs of people.

"Show your partner which one of the eight personality types you are like and give examples."

Which Personality Type Does God Love the Most?

Allow leaders to debate this point. Their answers will give you keen insight into their culture. Every culture tends to value one or two of the pictures of Christ more than the rest.

"God made each personality type and after He finished He said, 'It is good.' All of them are his favorite."

Which Personality Type Makes the Best Leader?

Ask leaders to discuss this question. Usually, two or three pictures of Christ will emerge as favorites. Leaders will argue these two or three personality types are best for a leader. We have found answers to vary significantly between Western and Eastern cultures. After the group communicates their thoughts, share the following insight with them.

"Many people are surprised to find out you can be an exceptional leader with any of the eight personality types. Leadership does not depend on personality. I could take you to eight mega-churches in America that have an attendance of over 5,000 people every week. Most people would say that these churches are led by great leaders. If you talked with the different pastors, you would discover each one had a different personality. Each one led with a different picture of Christ.

Personality is not what makes a good leader. A good leader is a person who can lead the whole team to work together and succeed. Jesus is the greatest leader of all time. Follow Him and you will become a great leader too."

Memory Verse

> *– Romans 12:4-5 – Just as each of us has one body with many members, and these members do not all have the same function, so in Christ we who are many form one body, and each member belongs to all the others.*

Everyone stands and says the memory verse ten times together. The first six times, they may use their Bible or student notes. The last four times, they say the verse from memory. Say the verse reference before quoting the verse each time and sit down when finished.

Following this routine will help the trainers know which teams have finished the lesson in the "Practice" section.

PRACTICE

Divide leaders into groups of four. Ask them to use the training process with the leadership lesson.

Walk leaders through the training process step-by-step, giving them 7-8 minutes to discuss each of the following sections.

Progress

"Share which one of the eight types of people you are most like and give examples."

Problems

"Share which one of the eight types of people you are least like and give examples."

Plans

"Share a simple plan to find out the different personality types in your group in the next month."

Everyone records each other's plans so they can pray for their partners later.

Practice

"Share one task that you will do in the next 30 days to help you improve as a leader in this area."

Everyone records their partners' practice item so they can pray for them later.

Leaders stand and say the memory verse ten times together after everyone has shared the skill they will practice.

Prayer

"Spend time praying for each other's plans and the skill you will practice the next 30 days to improve as a leader."

ENDING

The American Cheeseburger

"Ask leaders to pretend you are in a restaurant. Have leaders move into groups of three or four and explain their groups are "tables" where they are eating. Tell them you are the waiter and are going to take their order."

Drape a towel over your arm, go to the first table, and ask

them what they would like to eat. No matter what they order, say "Sorry, we are out of that right now, I will give you an American Cheeseburger instead."

After several tables, most people will order American Cheeseburgers because they realize that is all you have.

"This skit illustrates a common leadership mistake. Leaders expect everyone to act and be the same, but God has made each person different. Good leaders learn how to work with people with different personalities. They teach people how to cooperate and respect differences."

Ask one of the leaders to pray a prayer of thanksgiving for the different ways God has made people.

5

STRONGER TOGETHER

Leaders discovered their personality type in the last lesson. "Stronger Together," shows leaders how their personality type interacts with others. Why do people have eight different kinds of personalities in the world? Some say Noah's ark held eight people while others say God made a personality type for each point on the compass – north, northeast, east, etc. We can explain the reason simply. The world has eight different kinds of personalities because God created people in His image. If you want to see what God looks like, the Bible says to look at Jesus. The eight basic personality types in the world mirror the eight pictures of Jesus.

Jesus is like a soldier – commander in chief of God's army. He is like a seeker – seeking and saving the lost. He is like a shepherd – giving his followers food, water, and rest. Jesus is like a sower – sowing the Word of God in our lives. He is a son – God called him beloved and commanded us to listen to him. Jesus is the savior and calls us to represent Him in the world as saints. He is a servant – obedient to his Father, even to the point of death. Finally, Jesus is a steward – many parables are about managing time, money, or people.

Every leader carries the responsibility of helping people work together. Conflict inevitably occurs between different personalities because they view the world differently. The two most common ways people deal with conflict is to avoid or fight each other. A third way to deal with conflict, led by God's Spirit, is find solutions that respect and affirm each personality type.

The session ends with a drama contest that shows this truth in a humorous way. The "eight pictures of Christ" diagram aids us in understanding how to love others better. This is the job of all followers of Jesus.

PRAISE

Sing two worship songs together. Ask a leader to pray for this session.

PROGRESS

Ask another leader in the training to share a short testimony (three minutes) of how God is blessing his or her group. After the leader shares a testimony, ask the group to pray for him or her.

Alternatively, model a coaching time with a leader using the

"Progress, Problems, Plan, Practice, Prayer" leadership training model.

PROBLEM

"We learned about the eight different personality types in the last lesson. This knowledge helps us understand how conflict occurs in a group. Nothing stops a mission or ministry faster than conflict. People exchange heated words and hurt each other's feelings. Then, the mission or ministry begins to move in slow-motion."

PLAN

"Jesus is the Savior and calls His followers to be Saints representing Him to the world. The world knows we are Christians by how we handle conflict together. The plan for this lesson is to show you why conflict happens and how to handle disagreements when they come."

Why Are There Eight Kinds of People in the World?

> – *Genesis 1:26 – – Then God said, "Let us make man in our image, in our likeness. . . ."*

> – *Colossians 1:15 – – He (Jesus) is the image of the invisible God, the firstborn over all creation.*

"Man is created in the image of God. If you want to see the image of the invisible God, look at Jesus. Even in our fallen state, we reflect who Jesus is. There are eight pictures of Jesus in the Bible that help us know what Jesus is like."

What Is Jesus Like?

Soldier

> – – *Matthew 26:53 – – Or do you think that I cannot call on My Father, and He will provide Me at once with more than twelve legions of angels? (HCSB)*

> *Soldier – Raise sword.*

Seeker

> – *Luke 19:10 – – For the Son of Man came to seek and to save that which was lost." (NASB)*

> *Seeker – Look back and forth with hand above eyes.*

Shepherd

> – *John 10:11 – – I am the good shepherd. The good shepherd lays down his life for the sheep.*

> *Shepherd – Move arms toward your body as if you are gathering people.*

Sower

> – *Matthew 13:37 – – And He said, "The one who sows the good seed is the Son of Man, (NASB)*

> *Sower – Cast seeds with hands.*

Son or Daughter

> – *Luke 9:35 – – A voice came from the cloud, saying, "This is my Son, whom I have chosen; listen to him."*

Son – Move hands toward mouth as if you are eating.

Savior/Saint

– Mark 8:31 – He then began to teach them that the Son of Man must suffer many things and be rejected by the elders, chief priests and teachers of the law, and that he must be killed and after three days rise again.

"We are called to be saints who represent His saving work to the world"

Savior/Saint – Put hands in classic "praying hands" pose.

Servant

– John 13:14-15 – – Now that I, your Lord and Teacher, have washed your feet, you also should wash one another's feet. I have set you an example that you should do as I have done for you.

Servant – Wield a hammer.

Steward

– Luke 6:38 – "Give, and it will be given to you. A good measure, pressed down, shaken together and running over, will be poured into your lap. For with the measure you use, it will be measured to you."

Steward – Take money from shirt pocket or purse.

What Are the Three Choices We Have When Conflict Occurs?

Run away (flesh response)

"Different personalities have different ideas and ways of carrying out tasks. People directly across from each other on the circle diagram typically struggle working together the most. They usually labor to understand each other.

For example, the sower wants to spend money and time to see people grow, but the steward wants to save money and time so the mission can continue. Good decisions require both viewpoints. Stressing one over the other creates competition and poor judgment.

For most people, coping with conflict is difficult and the two parties end up not communicating. Fearing more conflict and hurt, we stay away from the other person. Our motto becomes 'Better safe than sorry.'

In this situation, people argue, run away, and hide from each other."

Hold fists together. Move them away from each other and behind your back.

Fight each other (flesh response)

"Sometimes people do not avoid conflict, but are openly hostile to the other person. We feel hurt or misunderstood and want the other person to 'pay' for what they have done. We may fight with words, attitudes, or our fists. A buildup of conflict always results.

For example, a seeker wants new experiences and opportunities, while a saint wants the group fixed on a solid foundation. We need both in the body of Christ. Two groups trying both 'new' and 'old' together can be challenging.

Worship styles seem particularly prone to this problem. Groups gather around their style and belittle other groups with a different style. Words, attitudes, and actions come against each other and unity suffers.

In this situation, we argue and fight against each other."

Hold fists together and hit them together.

Find a way by God's Spirit to work together (Spirit response)

"The Holy Spirit guides the third response. If we recognize that in our flesh we tend to flee or fight when it comes to conflict, we can ask and depend on the Spirit to help us find a way to work together. We believe that solutions to problems that come from the whole body of Christ are better. The third response takes communication, trust, love above all."

"For example, a soldier desires the church to be organized and on mission with God. A son or daughter, on the other hand, wants the church to be a healing place of family. The soldier concentrates on the task; the son or daughter concentrates on relationships.

As they unite in the Spirit, they find a way to carry out the mission and help everyone feel 'a part of the team.' We work, work, and work – but we also play, play, and play.

In this situation, we find a way to come together in Christ and work toward His kingdom."

Hold fists together, release fist and intertwine fingers, shake hands up and down, as if they are working together.

Memory Verse

> *– Galatians 2:20 – I have been crucified with Christ; and it is no longer I who live, but Christ lives in me; (NASB)*

Everyone stands and says the memory verse ten times together. The first six times, they may use their Bible or student notes. The last four times, they say the verse from memory. Say the verse reference before quoting the verse each time and sit down when finished.

Following this routine will help the trainers know which teams have finished the lesson in the "Practice" section.

PRACTICE

Drama Contest

Divide the leaders into groups of at least eight people each. Tell leaders you will arrange a drama contest with prizes for the winners. You will give first prize to the team that performs the funniest, true-to-life skit.

Each member of the group picks a picture of Christ to mimic. Leaders should choose a picture different from their own personality. For example, if a person's personality type is "soldier" they should choose another picture of Christ rather than "soldier" to act out in the drama.

The skit they will perform is "a group meeting about starting new churches in a neighboring province." Drama members should act out their role in conflict with one another (the flesh) only. No one is in the Spirit.

They will have 5 minutes to present their skit to the group. Urge them to "ham it up" so people will know which role they are acting out in the drama.

Give leaders enough time to practice their drama (at least 20 minutes).

Start the contest. At the end of each group's performance, go around the circle of actors and see if the leaders can guess what role each member was acting. Give "first place" to the group that was most humorous and true-to-life. Prize ideas: gospel tracts, worship CD, candy, etc.

After the groups have performed, ask each group to pick a few "all-stars" from their group. Ask the "all-stars" from each group to form a new group and have them perform the skit again as a newly formed "all-star" drama team.

A Common Question

What is the difference between the eight pictures of Christ and spiritual gifts?

God created people in His image, and if one wants to see the image of the invisible God, the Bible says to look at Jesus. The eight pictures are how people are "hard-wired" and true of both believers and unbelievers. Using the eight pictures as a framework for spiritual growth addresses a problem with spiritual gift inventories. How can an unbeliever take a spiritual gift inventory and discover they have spiritual gifts, though they do not believe in God at all?

The eight pictures of Christ are like "buckets" that spiritual gifts are poured into and released. A shepherd might have the spiritual gift of mercy, or exhortation, or giving, as the Spirit wills. We have observed that some spiritual gifts cluster around certain pictures of Christ more often than not. For example, the gift of serving and the picture of a servant often go together.

6

SHARE THE
GOSPEL

How can people believe if they have never heard the gospel? Unfortunately, followers of Jesus do not always share the gospel so that people can believe. One reason is they have never learned how to share the Gospel. Another reason is they get busy in their daily routine and forget to share.

In the "Share the Gospel" lesson, leaders learn how to make a "gospel bracelet" to share with friends and family. The bracelet reminds us to share with others and is a good conversation starter. The colors on the bracelet remind us how to share the gospel with people who are seeking God.

The gospel bracelet shows how we left God's family. In the beginning was God – the gold bead. The Holy Spirit created a perfect world with skies and seas – the blue bead. He created man and placed him in a beautiful garden – the green bead. The first man and woman disobeyed God and brought sin and suffering into the world – the black bead. God sent his only Son into the world and He lived a perfect life – the white bead. Jesus paid for our sins by dying on the cross – the red bead.

The gospel bracelet shows us how we can return to God's family by reversing the order. God has said anyone who believes Jesus died on the cross for them – the red bead – and that Jesus is the Son of God – the white bead – has their sins forgiven – the black bead. God adopts us back into His family and we grow more like Jesus – the green bead. God gives us his Holy Spirit – the blue bead – and promises we will be with him in heaven where there are streets of gold when we die – the gold bead.

The lesson closes showing that Jesus is the only way to God. No one is smart enough, good enough, strong enough, or loving enough to get to God by themselves. Jesus is the only path people may walk to return to God. Following Jesus is the only truth that sets people free from their sins. Only Jesus can grant everlasting life because of his death on the cross.

PRAISE

Sing two worship songs together. Ask a leader to pray for this session.

PROGRESS

Ask another leader in the training to share a short testimony (three minutes) of how God is blessing his or her group. After the leader shares a testimony, ask the group to pray for him or her.

PROBLEM

"Many believers struggle to share the gospel. They ask, 'Who should I share the gospel with?' and 'What should I say?' Believers often get busy and fail to recognize when God is working in another person's life to bring them to faith."

PLAN

"In this lesson, we will review a simple way to share the gospel, practice sharing it, and make a 'gospel bracelet' that will help us to remember to share the gospel often."

How Can I Share the Simple Gospel?

> – Luke 24:1-7 – On the first day of the week, very early in the morning, the women took the spices they had prepared and went to the tomb. They found the stone rolled away from the tomb, but when they entered, they did not find the body of the Lord Jesus. While they were wondering about this, suddenly two men in clothes that gleamed like lightning stood beside them. In their fright the women bowed down with their faces to the ground, but the men said to them, "Why do you look for the living among the dead? He is not here; he has risen! Remember how he told you, while he was still with you in Galilee: 'The Son of Man must be delivered over to the hands of sinners, be crucified and on the third day be raised again.'"

After leaders have read the scripture aloud, distribute the following supplies to each participant:

1. A gold, blue, green, black, white, and red bead

2. A piece of leather or cord twelve inches long

Explain how to make the "gospel bracelet." Begin by tying a knot in the middle of the cord to hold the beads in place. Thread each bead onto the bracelet as you explain its meaning.

gold bead

"In the beginning there was only God."

blue bead

"Then, the Spirit of God created everything in the world, including the seas and the skies."

green bead

"God made a beautiful garden, created man, and put him in God's family."

black bead

"Sadly, man disobeyed God and brought sin and suffering into the world. Because of his rebellion, man had to leave the garden and God's family."

white bead

"God still loved man very much, though, so He sent Jesus, His

Son, to the world. Jesus lived a perfect life and obeyed God in everything."

red bead

"Jesus died on the cross for our sins and was buried in a tomb."

At this point, leaders do not add beads to the gospel bracelet, but tie a knot to keep the beads in place. Begin the next section pointing to the red bead and working back until you end on the gold bead.

red bead

"God saw Jesus' sacrifice for our sins and accepted it. He resurrected Jesus from the grave after three days to show the world that Jesus is the only way back to God."

white bead

"Those who believe Jesus is God's Son and He has paid the price for their sins…"

black bead

"And those who repent of their sins and ask Jesus to help them…"

green bead

"…God forgives them and welcomes them back into His family, just like they were in the first garden."

blue bead

"God puts His Spirit in them and creates a new person, just like He created all of the world at the beginning."

gold bead

"Finally, all those who trust in Jesus will someday spend eternity with God. They will live with other believers in a city made of pure gold.

I like this bracelet because it reminds me where I have been and where I am going. The gospel bracelet also reminds me about how God has forgiven my sins and changed my life.

Are you ready to come back to God's family? Let's pray together and tell God you believe He created a perfect world and sent His Son to die for your sins. Repent of your sins, ask for forgiveness, and God will receive you into His family again."

Take a moment to ensure all leaders at the training are believers. After explaining the gospel bracelet, ask if anyone is ready to come back to God's family.

Why Do We Need Jesus' Help?

No one is smart enough to return to God.

> – Isaiah 55:9 – For as the heavens are higher than the earth, so are my ways higher than your ways, and my thoughts than your thoughts.

"Some people think many paths to God exist. They weave

elaborate theories to explain how Jesus could not possibly be the only way back to God. God's thoughts, however, make people's thoughts small-minded. When God says Jesus alone is the way, the truth, and the life, who will you believe?"

> *No one smart enough – Place index fingers of both hands to the side of your head and shake your head "No."*

No one is giving enough to return to God.

> *– Isaiah 64:6 – We are all infected and impure with sin. When we display our righteous deeds, they are nothing but filthy rags.*
>
> *Like autumn leaves, we wither and fall, and our sins sweep us away like the wind. (NLT)*

"Some people believe they can receive everlasting life by giving money to the poor. They think God will see their good deeds and allow them in heaven. Our best deeds, however, are as filthy rags compared with what God has done. He gave His only son on our behalf when Jesus died on the cross for our sins. God accepts this good deed alone for our salvation."

> *No one giving enough – Pretend to take a lot of money out of your shirt pocket or purse and shake your head "No."*

No one is strong enough to return to God.

> *– Romans 7:18 – For I know that nothing good lives in me, that is, in my flesh. For the desire to do what is good is with me, but there is no ability to do it. (HCSB)*

"Other people believe the way to God is through self-denial. They practice meditation, fasting, and reject the world. They believe, a person gains salvation by controlling his or her desires. A person must depend on his or her strength alone.

A drowning man does not have the power to save himself. He must receive help. Jesus is the only person strong enough to live a perfect life. We return to God by depending on Jesus' strength and not our own efforts."

> *No one strong enough – Hold both arms up in "strong man" position and shake your head "No."*

No one is good enough to return to God.

> *– Romans 3:23 – for all have sinned and fall short of the glory of God,*

"The last group of people believes they can get back to God because their good deeds outweigh their evil deeds. They are certain they have performed more good deeds and gained favor with God. They justify themselves, saying, "I've never done something as bad as that person over there."

God will judge all of us, however, against the perfect life of His Son Jesus. Compared with Jesus, all of us fall short. Only Jesus' sacrifice was good enough for God to accept. Only Jesus is good enough to bring us back into God's family. We must trust His goodness and not our own."

No one good enough – Put hands out as if balancing scales, move them up and down, and shake your head "No."

Memory Verse

– John 14:6 – Jesus answered, "I am the way and the truth and the life. No one comes to the Father except through me."

Everyone stands and says the memory verse ten times together. The first six times, they may use their Bible or student notes. The last four times, they say the verse from memory. Say the verse reference before quoting the verse each time and sit down when finished.

Following this routine will help the trainers know which teams have finished the lesson in the "Practice" section.

PRACTICE

Divide leaders into groups of four.

"Now we are going to use the same training process Jesus used to practice what we have learned in this leadership lesson."

Walk leaders through the training process step-by-step, giving them 7-8 minutes to discuss each of the following sections.

Progress

"Share a short testimony with your group about someone who has become a follower of Christ recently."

Problems

"Share with your group what makes sharing the gospel difficult for you."

Plans

"Share the names of five people with whom you will share the gospel in the next 30 days."

Everyone should record their partners' plans so they can pray for them later.

Practice

Using the "gospel bracelet" as a guide, each leader should take a turn sharing the gospel with their small group.

All group members stand and say the memory verse ten times together.

Prayer

"Spend time praying for the list of names in your group of people who need to come back to God's family."

ENDING

The Power of Training Trainers

Write the following table on a whiteboard or piece of poster paper before the session. Research the statistics before the session, but let leaders give their estimates. This debate should foster some active discussion about the correct numbers and make the numbers more "real" to participants.

	Total		Total
Population		Start New Churches	
Unbelievers		Avg. Church Size	
Believers		Total Churches	
Two % Reached		Church Goal	

"I would like to show you why Training Trees are important. Let's fill out the following table together."

[Statistics cited for the people group in this illustration are for example only. If all the leaders come from the same people group, use their people group statistics. If they come from several people groups, use province, state, or country numbers.]

"Our people group has a total population of 2,000,000 people. We estimate there are 5,000 believers, which means 1,995,000 people are not following Jesus. The goal is to reach at least 2% of the population for Jesus, which means 40,000 people. We still have a long way to go!

	Total		Total
Population	2,000,000	Start New Churches	10
Unbelievers	1,195,000	Avg. Church Size	50
Believers	5,000	Total Churches	100
Two % Reached	40,000	Church Goal	800

On average, an existing church will start a new church every 10 years. The average church size across the world is fifty people, so we estimate there are about 100 churches in our people group (5,000/50). Our goal is to reach 40,000 people, so we need to start 700 more churches. These figures are approximate, but help to form a picture of what is happening in our people group.

The average traditional church takes ten years to start another church, so in ten years we double the number of churches. Our goal for the total number of churches is 800 (40,000/50). Some churches will be much larger than fifty attenders, but many churches will be smaller, so this is a good estimate. Now let's compare two different ways of achieving our goal."

Traditional Churches	Years	Training Leaders	Years
100		5,000	
200	10	10,000	1
400	20	20,000	2
800	30	40,000	3

"As you can see, if we concentrate on training leaders to start groups, we can achieve our goal in three years. We currently have 5,000 believers. If each one shares the gospel, leads a person to Christ, trains them as leaders in a group, and teaches them how to do the same, we would double each year and have 40,000 believers after three years.

If we rely solely on starting churches the traditional way, we achieve our goal in 30 years. We currently have 100 churches and if they double every 10 years, we will have 800 churches in 30 years.

There is a big difference between three years and thirty years!

A common problem among churches is that they do not use a process to train people to become leaders. As a result, few leaders exist to help start new churches or new groups. When we train like Jesus, it solves this problem in a simple, but powerful way."

My Jesus Plan

Ask leaders to turn to the back of their participant guide where they will see "The Jesus Plan" page. Explain that leaders will share their Jesus Plan with the group at the end of the seminar. Afterwards, leaders will pray for God's blessing on their family, ministry, and plan.

"You will notice a place in the arrow to fill in the demographics for your target group. Take a few moments to pray and fill in the blanks as best as you can. You can always change them later if you receive better information."

7

MAKE DISCIPLES

A good leader always has a good plan. Jesus gave the disciples a simple, but powerful, plan for their ministries in Luke 10: prepare your heart, find people of peace, share the good news, and evaluate the results. Jesus has given us a good plan to follow.

Whether we start a ministry in a church, a new church, or a cell group, the steps in the Jesus Plan will help us avoid unnecessary mistakes. This lesson teaches leaders how to coach each other on their personal Jesus Plans. They will also begin working toward their Jesus Plan presentations to the group.

PRAISE

Sing two worship songs together. Ask a leader to pray for this session.

PROGRESS

Ask another leader in the training to share a short testimony (three minutes) of how God is blessing his or her group. After the leader shares a testimony, ask the group to pray for him or her.

Alternatively, model a coaching time with a leader using the "Progress, Problems, Plan, Practice, Prayer" leadership training model.

PROBLEM

"When we fail to plan, we plan to fail. Developing a simple, strategic plan can be difficult. Many leaders spend most of their time reacting to problems rather than running on a clear track to the future."

PLAN

"Jesus came to seek and save the lost and when we follow Him, we will do the same. He gave the disciples a clear plan that we can also apply to our mission."

What is the First Step in Jesus' Plan?

– Luke 10:1-4 – After this the Lord appointed seventy-two others and sent them two by two ahead of him to every town and place where he was about to go.

He told them, "The harvest is plentiful, but the workers are few. Ask the Lord of the harvest, therefore, to send out workers into his harvest field.

Go! I am sending you out like lambs among wolves.

Do not take a purse or bag or sandals; and do not
greet anyone on the road.

1. Prepare Your Hearts (1-4)

Go in Pairs (1)

"In verse one, Jesus says to go in pairs: in most cultures, that means two men or two women. Without a partner, you are alone. One times one times one still equals one. Two times two times two equals eight, however. The potential for multiplication increases with a partner.

Hard times discourage people, especially if they work alone. Throughout the Bible, spiritual leaders worked with partners and Jesus reaffirmed this practice in His plan."

Teach this principle by performing the following skit:

Lean on Me

"What might happen if you went somewhere to minister alone and had an accident?"

Walk around the room as if you are going to your ministry area. Tell everyone you were in an accident and have broken your leg. Limp around the room while trying to minister to others. Then announce lightning has struck you. Continue trying to minister, but now twitch your neck.

"How might events be different if a partner joined me?"

Repeat the same scenario but with a partner this time. Your partner helps bandage and care for you after the accident.

Your partner warns you to stay out of the rain when you have a metal rod in your hand.

"Jesus is wise when He says to go in pairs. He knows that troubles will come, and we will need someone to help us when they do."

Use index and middle fingers on both hands to "walk" together.

"Write in the first column of "My Jesus Plan" the person you believe will be your partner."

Go Where Jesus is at Work (1)

"Because we follow Jesus, we do nothing by ourselves, but look to see where Jesus is working, and join Him. Seeing where Jesus wants us to go is not always easy. The good news, though, is He loves us and will show us."

Review hand motions from the "Go" lesson from the Discipleship Seminar.

"I do nothing by myself."

Put one hand over heart and shake head 'no'.

"I look to see where God is working."

Put one hand over eyes, search left and right.

"Where He is working, I join Him."

Point hand toward a place in front of you and shake head yes.

"And I know He loves me and will show me."

Raise hands upwards in praise and then cross them over your heart.

"Write in the first column of "My Jesus Plan" where God is working and where He is calling you to go."

Pray for Leaders from the Harvest (2)

"In verse two, Jesus commands us to pray for the work before we go. Jesus prayed fervently before carrying out His plan. We should also spend much time in prayer before we begin our plan."

When we pray, we praise God for the people on our team, for how he is working, and for the people we will reach."

Praise – Hands raised in worship.

"We repent of sin in our lives. We repent for any sins in the lives of people who are following us. We repent also for any sins of the group we are reaching (superstition, idol worship, or use of amulets for example)."

Repent – Palms are outward shielding the face; head turned away.

"Then we ask God to give us local leaders in the place we are going. We ask God to make us leaders who follow Jesus, so when others follow us, they are following Jesus."

Ask – Hands cupped to receive.

"Finally, we yield to what God wants us to do."

Yield – Hands folded in prayer and placed high on the forehead to symbolize respect.

"Write in the first column of "My Jesus Plan" the names of potential leaders you are praying for in the place you are going."

Go Humbly (3)

"In verse three, Jesus said He is sending us as lambs among wolves, so we go humbly. People will listen to a message that comes from a humble heart. They will not listen if they believe us to be proud or arrogant."

Teach this principle by performing the following skit

The Big Leader

"What do you think people in a village would think if I came to their village like this…?"

Walk around with your chest puffed out saying, "I'm the Big Leader, you must listen to me!" Let everyone know that you think you are the biggest and the best.

"Jesus is wise when He says to go humbly. People are more receptive when the messenger is humble and has a heart to help others. No one likes a bossy person."

Go humbly – Put hands in "praying hand" position and bow.

"Write in the first column of "My Jesus Plan" the answer to the following question: what does 'go humbly' mean to you?"

Depend on God, not Money (4)

"In The Jesus Plan, Jesus gives us clear principles to follow when we start a ministry or mission. Throughout Christian history, leaders have made many mistakes in ministry because they ignored one of these principles. Jesus tells us that our ministry or mission must depend on God and not money. We can serve God or money, but not both. We should make sure that everything we do depends on God and not money."

Teach this principle by performing the following skit:

Money is Like Honey

"What do you think people in a village would think if we came to their village like this…?"

Carry a bag with you and pretend you have entered a village. Approach one of the leaders and say, "We're starting a new church in the village. We have tons of money. Come and see what we can do for you!" Repeat this same speech to several leaders in the group.

"Jesus is wise when He says not to trust in money. In ministry, people should come to Jesus because He is the son of God and Savior of the world, not because of promises of money and help. Money is like honey and attracts trouble if we depend on it and not God."

Depend on God, Not Money – Pretend to take money from your shirt pocket,
shake your head "no," and then point toward heaven shaking your head "yes."

"Write in the first column of "My Jesus Plan" how much it will cost the first year to fund your new ministry or mission."

Go directly to where He is calling (4)

"Jesus commands us in verse four not to greet anyone along the road. He is not commanding us to be rude, but to stay focused on the mission He has given us. Most of us easily become sidetracked by doing good tasks, rather than doing the best tasks."

Teach this principle by performing the following skit:

Good Distractions

"What do you think people in a village would think if I came to their village like this...?"

Tell everyone the apprentice is going to show this principle. Point to a group at the other end of the room and say:

"A group of people have asked my friend to come help them. Watch what happens."

The apprentice describes to the leaders what he is doing as he does it. The apprentice sets off toward the group of people needing help, but remembers he should say good-bye to his friends. He sits with his friends and talks with them for a while. After a few minutes, he "remembers" he needs to go on a mission. He gets up to start again, but remembers that he owes his sister some money, so he goes to her house. She feeds him dinner and asks him to stay the night. The third time he sets off, he makes another culturally fitting excuse. Finally, he gets to the ministry area, but no one in the village wants to listen to him now.

"Jesus is wise when he tells us to go directly to the place of ministry to which he has called us. The cares of this world can easily distract us and cause us to miss what God is doing in a ministry place."

> *Place palms and fingers from both hands together and make a "straight away" motion.*

"Write in the first column of "My Jesus Plan" a list of possible distractions that you might face in your notes."

Memory Verse

> *– Luke 10:2 – He told them, "The harvest is plentiful, but the workers are few. Ask the Lord of the harvest, therefore, to send out workers into his harvest field."*

Everyone stands and says the memory verse ten times together. The first six times, they may use their Bible or student notes. The last four times, they say the verse from memory. Say the verse reference before quoting the verse each time and sit down when finished.

Following this routine will help the trainers know which teams have finished the lesson in the "Practice" section.

PRACTICE

Divide leaders into groups of four. Ask them to use the training process with this leadership lesson and answer the questions below.

Walk leaders through the training process step-by-step, giving them 7-8 minutes to discuss each of the following sections.

Progress

"Which part of this step is the easiest for your group to obey?"

Problems

"Which part of this step is the hardest for your group to obey?"

Plans

"What is one task you will start doing in your group in the next 30 days to obey this step of The Jesus Plan?"

Everyone should record each other's plans so they can pray for their partners later.

Practice

"What is one task you will improve in your group in the next 30 days to obey this step of The Jesus Plan?"

Everyone records their partners' practice item so they can pray for them later.

Leaders stand and say the memory verse ten times together after everyone has shared the skill they will practice.

Prayer

Spend time praying for each other's plans

ENDING

My Jesus Plan

Ask leaders to turn in the back of their participant guide to "The Jesus Plan" page.

"Using your notes from this session, fill out the first column of your Jesus Plan – how you will do your work. Write specific details about how you will follow Jesus' principles for ministry in Luke 10."

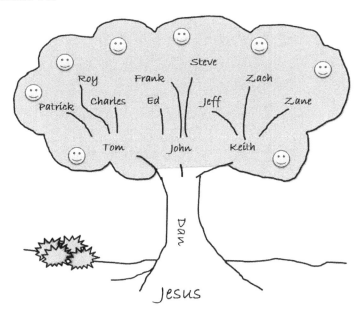

8

START GROUPS

Leaders prepare their hearts in Step 1 of the Jesus Plan. The lesson "Start Groups" covers steps 2, 3, and 4. We could avoid many mistakes in ministry and mission simply by following the principles of Jesus' plan in Luke 10. Leaders apply these principles at the end of the session as they fill out their personal "Jesus Plan."

Step 2 is about developing relationships. We join God where He is working and find influential people who are responsive to the message. We eat and drink what they give us to show them acceptance. We do not move from one friendship to another because this discredits the message of reconciliation we preach.

We share the good news in Step 3. Jesus is a shepherd and wants to protect and provide for people. In this step, trainers encourage leaders to find ways to bring healing as they minister. People do not care what you know until they know that you care. Healing the sick opens doors to share the Gospel.

We evaluate the results and adjust in Step 4. How receptive are the people? Is there genuine interest in spiritual matters or another reason like money driving their curiosity? If people are responding, we stay and continue the mission. If people are not responding, Jesus commands us to leave and start somewhere else.

PRAISE

Sing two worship songs together. Ask a leader to pray for this session.

PROGRESS

Ask another leader in the training to share a short testimony (three minutes) of how God is blessing his or her group. After the leader shares a testimony, ask the group to pray for him or her.

Alternatively, model a coaching time with a leader using the "Progress, Problems, Plan, Practice, Prayer" leadership training model.

PROBLEM

"Many times believers have a good heart and are passionate about reaching their community. They do not have a simple plan to follow that fits their aims, however. Many start groups by trial-and-error, but this method wastes time and energy.

Jesus gave the disciples clear instructions about how to start groups. When we follow His plan, we join Him where He is working and avoid needless mistakes."

PLAN

"The goal for this lesson is to show you a good way to start a disciple group following Jesus' instructions. We start by finding a person of peace and meeting their physical and spiritual needs. Jesus also commands us to evaluate our work at the end of His plan."

– Luke 10:2–4 – He told them, "The harvest is plentiful, but the workers are few. Ask the Lord of the harvest, therefore, to send out workers into his harvest field."

What is the Second Step in Jesus' Plan?

– Luke 10:5-8 – "When you enter a house, first say, 'Peace to this house.'

If a man of peace is there, your peace will rest on him; if not, it will return to you.

Stay in that house, eating and drinking whatever they give you, for the worker deserves his wages. Do not move around from house to house.

"When you enter a town and are welcomed, eat what is set before you.

2. Develop Friendships (5-8)

Find a Person of Peace (5, 6)

"In verses five and six, Jesus commands us to find people of peace. A person of peace is someone who is seeking God in the place you are going. When you talk to them about spiritual matters, they express interest and want to learn more. God is already working and drawing this person to Himself. Sharing our testimony is often a good way to find the person of peace."

Write in the second column of your Jesus plan 'People of Peace' you are aware of in your target area.

Person of Peace – Clasp hands together as if friends are shaking hands.

Eat and drink what they give you (7, 8)

"Why do you think Jesus says 'eat and drink what they give you' in verse seven? He wants us to be culturally sensitive as we develop friendships. The best way to do this is to eat and drink what your host gives you in friendship.

Sometimes, you may have to ask for God's grace when some unusual food turns your stomach! Nevertheless, if you ask, you will receive. Remember, people feel loved and accepted when we eat what they eat and drink what they drink."

Write in the second column of your Jesus plan any customs or food preferences of your target group to which you will need to be sensitive.

Eat and Drink – Pretend to eat and drink. Then rub stomach as if the food is good.

Do not move from house to house (7)

"In verse seven, Jesus says to remain in the home of the person we connect with in the village. Friendships take time to develop and every relationship deals with conflict and trouble from time to time. If we move at the first sign of trouble, it discredits the message of reconciliation we are preaching."

Don't move from house to house – Make the outline of a roof of a house with both hands. Move the house to several places and shake head, "No."

Teach the principles in the second step of Jesus' plan by performing the following skit:

How to Make a Village Angry

"What do you think people in a village would think if we came into their village like this?"

Tell everyone that you and your partner have followed The Jesus Plan so far. You are going to a ministry site in pairs. You have prayed, you are going humbly, and you are not depending on money. God is working in the village and the two of you have gone straight there. Tell them to watch what happens now and see how the villagers respond.

Ask leaders to imagine the training group is a village. Clusters of people are houses in the village.

Go to the first house, give a blessing, sit down with them, and spend time with them. Ask them if you can have something to eat because you are extremely hungry. After your guests bring food to you, eat it, and make a sour face. Then, tell your partner that you cannot stay there any longer because the food is so bad, and you think you are going to die. Say good-bye while rubbing your stomach as if you have a stomachache.

Go to the second house, give a blessing, sit down with them, and again agree to spend the night. "Pretend" to go to sleep. After a while, your partner tells you he cannot stay there any longer because a man in the house snores so loudly. Your partner did not get any sleep all night. Say good-bye while rubbing your eyes.

Go to the third house, give a blessing, sit down with them, and stay awhile. The next day, tell your partner you cannot stay there any longer because they gossip so much that it hurts your ears. Say good-bye and leave, rubbing your ears.

Go to the final house, give a blessing, sit down with them, and stay awhile. Tell everyone you have heard that this house has beautiful daughters. You are trying to help your friend find a wife. Tell the members of the household all of the amazing qualities of your partner. Explain you are sure God wants your partner to marry one of their beautiful daughters.

"If we tried to share the gospel in this village, what would the villagers think? They would think we had no honor. All we cared about was what they could give to us. Following The Jesus Plan helps us avoid many mistakes."

Write in the second column of your Jesus plan how you will contribute to the household in which you stay. What are some specific ways you can be a blessing to them?

What is the Third Step in Jesus' Plan?

> – Luke 10:9 – Heal the sick who are there and tell them,
> 'The kingdom of God is near you.'

3. Share the Good News

Heal the sick (9)

"The ministry of Jesus included ministry to both physical and spiritual needs. We can bring healing to a village or group of people in many ways, such as by doing community development, improving the water supply, bringing medical or dental help, praying for the sick, and counseling."

Write in the second column of your Jesus plan a practical way you can meet physical needs in the community through your ministry or mission.

> *Heal the sick − Extend arms as if you were laying hands on a person who is ill for healing.*

Share the gospel (9)

"The second part of sharing the good news is sharing the gospel."

Review the Gospel using the Gospel bracelet

"Good news is only good news if people can understand it in their context. An important aspect of proclaiming the gospel is making sure that it makes sense to those who hear it."

> *Share the Gospel − Cup hands around mouth as if you were holding a megaphone.*

Teach the principles in the third step of Jesus' strategy by performing the following skit:

The Two-Winged Bird

"Jesus said to heal the sick and preach the gospel. It is like two wings on a bird. You need both to fly!"

Ask for a volunteer. Explain the volunteer is a gifted evangelist and you work best healing the sick.

Ask the volunteer to hold up both arms like he has wings. Explain his right arm is strong in evangelism, but his left arm is weaker (ask him to make his left arm smaller than his right arm).

Hold up both of your arms like you have wings. Explain that your left arm is strong in healing the sick, but your right arm is weaker. You are weak at sharing the gospel. Ask the volunteer to fly with his strong and weak wings. You do the same. (Both of you should twirl around in circles)

"How could the results be different if we decided to work together?"

Join your "weak" arm (evangelism) to the "weak" arm of the volunteer (healing the sick).

"When we put our strengths together and work side-by-side, we can fly."

You and the volunteer flap your "strong" arms together and "fly" around the room.

What is the Fourth Step in Jesus' Plan?

> – Luke 10:10-11 – But when you enter a town and are not welcomed, go into its streets and say, 'Even the dust of your

town that sticks to our feet we wipe off against you. Yet be sure
of this: The kingdom of God is near.'

4. Evaluate the Results and Adjust

Evaluate how they respond (10, 11)

"A key to long-term success in any mission is the ability to evaluate. In this step, Jesus tells us to analyze the way people are responding and make corrections to our plans.

Sometimes people do not respond because they do not understand our message and we need to make it clearer. Other times people do not respond because they have sin in their lives, so we share God's forgiveness with them. Still others are not receptive because of negative experiences in their past and we love them back to the family of God. A time comes, however, when we must evaluate the openness of the people we are working with and adjust our plan accordingly.

A key step in the Jesus Plan is deciding before we start how we will evaluate the results."

Write in the second column of your Jesus plan what "success" in this mission or ministry will look like? How will you evaluate their response?

> *Evaluate results – Hold palms outward as if balancing scales. Move the scales up and down with a questioning look on your face.*

Leave if they do not respond (11)

"The last principle in the Jesus Plan is difficult for many people. We should leave the place we are ministering if they do not respond. Many times, we continue to believe something will change. We keep hoping when it is time to move on."

"A strategic part of mission work is determining when it is time to move on. Some want to leave too quickly, others too slowly. Leaving friendships is never easy, but it is important to remember that Jesus commanded us to move on if people are not responding.

How much time should you invest in people before you decide they are not going to respond: one day, one month or one year? Every ministry setting is different. The reality is that many people stay too long and miss the blessing of God in another place because they weren't obedient to the principles in the Jesus Plan."

Write in the second column of your Jesus plan how long you think you will need to stay to carry out the mission God has given to you. If this group of people is not responsive to the gospel, where will you start next?

Leave if no results – Wave good-bye.

Memory Verse

– Luke 10:9 – Heal the sick who are there and tell them, "The kingdom of God is near you."

Everyone stands and says the memory verse ten times together. The first six times, they may use their Bible or student notes. The last four times, they say the verse from memory. Say the verse reference before quoting the verse each time and sit down when finished.

Following this routine will help the trainers know which teams have finished the lesson in the "Practice" section.

PRACTICE

Divide leaders into groups of four. Ask them to use the training process with the leadership lesson.

Walk leaders through the training process step-by-step, giving them 7-8 minutes to discuss each of the following sections.

Progress

"Which part of these steps are the easiest for your group to obey?"

Problems

"Which part of these steps are the hardest for your group to obey?"

Plans

"What is one task you will start doing in your group in the next 30 days to obey these steps of The Jesus Plan?"

Leaders should record each other's plans so they can pray for their partners later.

Practice

"What is one task you will improve in your group in the next 30 days to obey these steps of The Jesus Plan?"

Everyone records their partners' practice item so they can pray for them later.

Leaders stand and say the memory verse ten times together after everyone has shared the skill they will practice.

Prayer

Spend time praying for each other's plans. Pray that God will continue to help the groups progress and strengthen their weak areas.

ENDING

My Jesus Plan

Ask leaders to turn in the back of their participant guide to "The Jesus Plan" page.

"Using your notes from this session, fill out the second and third columns of your Jesus Plan. These columns indicate who our people of peace are, and how we will minister to them. Write specific details about how you will follow Jesus' principles for ministry in Luke 10."

9

MULTIPLY
GROUPS

Healthy reproducing churches are the result of growing
strong in God, sharing the gospel, making disciples, starting
groups, and training leaders. Most leaders have never started
a church, however, and do not know how to begin. "Multiply
Groups" introduces the places we should focus on when we
start groups that lead to churches.

In the book of Acts, Jesus commands us to start groups in
four different areas. He says to start groups in the city and
the region where we live. Then, He says to start new fellow-
ships in a neighboring region and different ethnic group from
where we live. Finally, Jesus commands us to go to faraway
places and reach every ethnic group in the world. Trainers
encourage leaders to adopt Jesus' heart for all peoples and
make plans to reach their Jerusalem, Judea, Samaria, and to the

ends of the world. Leaders add these commitments to their "Jesus Plan."

The book of Acts also describes the work of four kinds of group starters. Peter, a pastor, helped start a group in the house of Cornelius. Paul, a layperson, traveled throughout the Roman Empire starting groups. Priscilla & Aquila, self-employed business owners, started groups wherever their business took them. "Persecuted" people in Acts 8 scattered and started groups wherever they went.

In this lesson, leaders identify possible group starters in their stream of influence and add them to their "Jesus Plan." The session ends by addressing the assumption that starting churches needs a big bank account. Most churches start in homes with little more expense than a Bible.

PRAISE

Sing two worship songs together. Ask a leader to pray for this session.

PROGRESS

Ask another leader in the training to share a short testimony (three minutes) of how God is blessing his or her group. After the leader shares a testimony, ask the group to pray for him or her.

Alternatively, model a coaching time with a leader using the "Progress, Problems, Plan, Practice, Prayer" leadership training model.

PROBLEM

"Leading an existing group or church is not easy. The thought of starting another group or church seems impossible. Churches struggle with how to use limited money, time, or people. Jesus knows our stewardship needs, however, and still commands us to start new churches.

Another problem we face when starting groups or churches is the fact that most believers have never started a group or church. Pastors, leaders, businesspeople, and church members have a picture in mind of what it takes to be a "real" church. This most often translates into starting churches that look exactly like the mother church, but this almost guarantees that the new church will fail."

PLAN

"Do you remember when we talked about how to go from 5,000 to 40,000 believers? The key to that growth is every believer starting a new group. In this lesson, we will learn the four areas we should start groups. Then, we will identify four types of people who started groups in the book of Acts."

Where Are the Four Places Jesus Commanded Believers to Start Groups?

> – Acts 1:8 – But you will have power, when the Holy Spirit has come on you; and you will be my witnesses in Jerusalem and all Judaea and Samaria, and to the ends of the earth.

Jerusalem

"Jesus told the disciples to start groups in the same city where they lived and among the same ethnic group. When we follow His example, we will start new groups and churches in the cities where we live."

In column three of your Jesus Plan, write the name of a place in the city you live that needs a new group or church. Write a short description about how this will happen.

Judea

"Second, Jesus told the disciples to start groups in the same region where they lived. Jerusalem was an urban setting, while Judea was a rural part of Israel. The people living in Judea were the same ethnic group as the disciples. Following Jesus' command, we will start new groups and churches in the rural areas where we live."

In column three of your Jesus Plan, write the name of a place in the same region you live that needs a new group or church. Write a short description about how this will happen.

Samaria

"Third, Jesus commanded the disciples to start groups in a different city with a different ethnic group. The Jewish people despised the people who lived in Samaria. In spite of their prejudices, Jesus called the disciples to share the good news and start groups and churches among the Samaritans. We follow Jesus' command when we start groups or churches in the cities close to us among a different ethnic group."

In column three of your Jesus Plan, write the name of a place in a different city with a different ethnic group that needs a new group or church. Write a short description about how this will happen.

Uttermost

"Finally, Jesus commissioned the disciples to start groups throughout the world and among all the different ethnic groups on the earth. Obeying this command typically requires learning a new language and new culture. We obey this command when we send missionaries from our church to start new groups and churches in foreign places."

In column three of your Jesus Plan, write the name of a place in a different region with a different ethnic group that needs a new group or church. Write a short description about how this will happen.

What Are Four Ways to Start a Group or Church?

Peter

> – Acts 10:9 – The next day as Cornelius's messengers were
> nearing the town, Peter went up on the flat roof to pray.
> It was about noon, (NLT)

"Peter pastored the church in Jerusalem. Cornelius asked him to come to Joppa to share the good news of Jesus Christ. When Peter shared with Cornelius' household, everyone received Christ, came back to God's family, and a new group started.

One way to start new groups or churches is for a pastor of an existing church to go on a short-term mission trip and help start a new group or church. This kind of church-planting assignment usually requires one to three weeks."

In column four of your Jesus Plan, write the name of a pastor you know who might help start a new group or church. Write a short description about how this will happen.

Paul

> – Acts 13:2 – While they were ministering to the Lord and fasting, the Holy Spirit said, "Set apart for Me Barnabas and Saul for the work to which I have called them." (NASB)

"Paul and Barnabas were leaders in the church at Antioch. God spoke to them during a worship time and commissioned them to go to unreached areas and share the gospel. In obedience, they started groups and churches throughout the Roman Empire.

The second way to start groups or churches is to send leaders out to other cities and regions to share the gospel. These missionaries gather new believers and start new groups or churches. This mission assignment typically requires one to three months."

In column four of your Jesus Plan, write the name of church leaders you know who might help start a new group or church. Write a short description about how this will happen.

Priscilla & Aquila

> – I Corinthians 16:19 – The churches in the province of Asia send you greetings. Aquila and Priscilla greet you warmly in the Lord, and so does the church that meets at their house.

"Priscilla and Aquila were business people in the church. They started a group or church wherever they lived and worked. When their business moved, they started a new group or church in their new location.

The third way to start new groups or churches is for Christian business people to start groups that become churches among their clientele. If a Christian businessperson moves to an area where no church exists, they start a group. This mission assignment typically requires one to three years."

In column four of your Jesus Plan, write the name of business people you know who might help start a new group or church. Write a short description about how this will happen.

Persecuted

> – Acts 8:1 – And Saul was one of the witnesses, and he agreed completely with the killing of Stephen. A great wave of persecution began that day, sweeping over the church in Jerusalem; and all the believers except the apostles were scattered through the regions of Judea and Samaria. (NLT)

"The last group of people who started groups and churches in the book of Acts was persecuted believers. Many believers fled Jerusalem when Saul began violently to persecute the Church. They started groups and churches throughout Judaea and Samaria. We know this to be true, because the apostles later visited churches already set up in those areas.

The final way to start new groups and churches is with persecuted believers who must move to a new town. If no group or church exists, newly arrived believers start one. Starting a group or church does not require a seminary degree, just a love for Jesus, and a heart that wants to obey His commands."

In column four of your Jesus Plan, write the name of displaced people you know who might help start a new group or church. Write a short description about how this will happen.

Memory Verse

> – Acts 1:8 – But you will receive power when the Holy Spirit comes on you; and you will be my witnesses in Jerusalem, and in all Judea and Samaria, and to the ends of the earth."

Everyone stands and says the memory verse ten times together. The first six times, they may use their Bible or student notes. The last four times, they say the verse from memory. Say the verse reference before quoting the verse each time and sit down when finished.

Following this routine will help the trainers know which teams have finished the lesson in the "Practice" section.

PRACTICE

Divide leaders into groups of four. Ask them to use the training process with the leadership lesson.

Walk leaders through the training process step-by-step, giving them 7-8 minutes to discuss each of the following sections.

Progress

"Share progress you have made in starting groups or churches in the four different places with four different kinds of group starters."

Problems

"Share problems you are having starting groups or churches in the four different places with the four different kinds of group starters."

Plans

"Share two tasks you will lead your group to do in the next 30 days that will help them start a new group or church."

Everyone records each other's plans so they can pray for their partners later.

Practice

"Share one task that you will do in the next 30 days to help you improve as a leader in this area."

Everyone records their partners' practice item so they can pray for them later.

Leaders stand and say the memory verse ten times together after everyone has shared the skill they will practice.

Prayer

Spend time praying for each other's plans and the skill you will practice the next 30 days to improve as a leader.

ENDING

How Much Does It Cost to Start a New Church?

"What do you need to start a new church? Let's make a list."

Write a list on the whiteboard as students answer the question. Allow for discussion and debate. For example, if someone says "a building," ask the rest of the students if a building is necessary to start a church.

"Now that we have a list of the items you need to start a church, let's put a price by each item."

Go down the list asking students to estimate the cost of each item. Encourage learners to discuss and agree on one price for each line. Typically, the group will decide it costs nothing to start a new church, or at the most, enough money to buy one Bible.

"The purpose of this exercise is to address a common mistake people make when planning to start churches. They assume it takes a lot of money to start a church. Most churches, however, start in homes and do not cost much money. Even the large mega-churches of today typically started in a home. Faith, hope, and love are the only essentials to start a church, not a big bank account."

My Jesus Plan

Ask leaders to turn in the back of their participant guide to "The Jesus Plan" page.

"We will present our Jesus Plans to one another in the next

session. Take a few minutes to complete you Jesus plan and think about how you will present it to the group. When you finish, spend some time in prayer asking God's blessing on the next session."

Another Common Question

How do you work with non-literate people at training sessions?

Follow Jesus Training uses several teaching aids that help literate and non-literate people remember what they have learned. In our experience, both groups enjoy and benefit alike from the training. We highlight the hand motions more when training non-literate people. In some Asian cultures, women receive no education past the third-grade level. After training such a group of women, they approached us with tears in their eyes. "Thank you," they said, "because the hand motions helped us learn, and we can now follow Jesus."

Even in a non-literate setting, usually one person can read for the group. Typically, we ask this person to read the Scriptures aloud for the whole group. Sometimes we ask the reader to say the Scriptures 2 or 3 times to make sure the group understands. If we know ahead of time the group is mainly non-literate, we arrange to produce a video or audio recording of each session.

Television and radio heavily influence non-literate people, even in faraway villages. Do not make the mistake of thinking you have to teach the lesson repeatedly to non-literate learners. If learners do not understand the lesson the first time, train them an additional time, and then leave a recording or video for them to review when you are not there. Most places have at least a public DVD or VCD player available. MP3 players are readily accessible and can run on batteries.

God will continue to bless many learners after you have left through video and audio recordings. If you produce a video or audio recording, please send a copy to *info@TheFollowJesusProject.com*.

10

FOLLOW JESUS

Leaders have learned in *Training Radical Leaders* who builds the church and why that is important. They have mastered the five parts of Jesus' strategy to reach the world and practiced coaching one another. They understand the seven qualities of a great leader, have developed a "Training Tree" for the future, and know how to work with different personalities. Each leader has a plan based on Jesus' plan in Luke 10. "Follow Jesus" addresses the one part of leadership that remains: motivation.

Two thousand years ago, people followed Jesus for various reasons. Some, like James and John, believed following Jesus would bring them fame. Others, like the Pharisees, followed Him to criticize and show their superiority. Still others, like Judas, followed Jesus for money. A crowd of five thousand wanted to follow Jesus because He provided the food they needed. Another group followed Jesus because they needed healing, and only one person returned to say thank you. Sadly, many people selfishly followed Jesus for what He could give them. Today is no different. As leaders, we should examine ourselves and ask, "Why am I following Jesus?"

Jesus praised people who followed Him from a heart of love. The extravagant gift of perfume by a spurned woman carried the promise of remembrance wherever people preached the gospel. A widow's mite touched Jesus' heart more than all the gold of the temple. Jesus was disappointed when a promising young man refused to love God with his whole heart, choosing his riches instead. Also, Jesus only asked Peter one question to restore him after his betrayal, "Simon, do you love me?" Spiritual leaders love people and love God.

The session finishes with each leader sharing their "Jesus Plan." Leaders pray for one another, commit to working together, and coaching new leaders for the love and glory of God.

PRAISE

Sing two worship songs together. Ask a leader to pray for this session.

PROGRESS

Welcome

Who Builds the Church?

Why is That Important?

How does Jesus Build His Church?

Train like Jesus

How Did Jesus Train Leaders?

Memory Verse

> – I Corinthians 11:1 – Be imitators of me, just as
> I also am of Christ. (NASB)

Lead like Jesus

Who Did Jesus Say Is The Greatest Leader?

What are Seven Qualities of a Great Leader?

Memory Verse

> – John 13:14-15 – Now that I, your Lord and Teacher, have
> washed your feet, you also should wash one another's feet. I
> have set you an example that you should do
> as I have done for you.

Grow Strong

Which Personality Has God Given You?

Which Personality Type does God like the Most?

Which Personality Type makes the Best Leader?

Memory Verse

– Romans 12:4-5 – Just as each of us has one body with many members, and these members do not all have the same function, so in Christ we who are many form one body, and each member belongs to all the others.

Stronger Together

Why Are There Eight Kinds Of People In The World?

What is Jesus like?

What Are The Three Choices We Have When Conflict Occurs?

Memory Verse

– Galatians 2:20 – I have been crucified with Christ; and it is no longer I who live, but Christ lives in me; (NASB)

Share the Gospel

How Can I Share the Simple Gospel?

Why Do We Need Jesus' Help?

Memory Verse

– *John 14:6-Jesus answered, "I am the way and the truth and the life. No one comes to the Father except through me."*

Make Disciples

What is the First Step in Jesus' Plan?

Memory Verse

– *Luke 10:2– He told them, "The harvest is plentiful, but the workers are few. Ask the Lord of the harvest, therefore, to send out workers into his harvest field."*

Start Groups

What is the Second Step in Jesus' Plan?

What is the Third Step in Jesus' Plan?

What is the Fourth Step in Jesus' Plan?

Memory Verse

– *Luke 10:9 – Heal the sick who are there and tell them, 'The kingdom of God is near you.'*

Start Churches

Where are the four places Jesus commanded believers to start churches?

What are four ways to start a church?

How much does it cost to start a new church?

Memory Verse

– Acts 1:8 – But you will receive power when the Holy Spirit comes on you; and you will be my witnesses in Jerusalem, and in all Judea and Samaria, and to the ends of the earth.

PLAN

Why do you Follow Jesus?

"When Jesus walked this earth two thousand years ago, people followed Him for different reasons.

People like James and John believed following Jesus would bring them fame."

– Mark 10:35-37 – James and John, the two sons of Zebedee, came up to Jesus, saying, "Teacher, we want You to do for us whatever we ask of You." And He said to them, "What do you want Me to do for you?" They said to Him, "Grant that we may sit, one on Your right and one on Your left, in Your glory." (NASB)

"People like the Pharisees followed Jesus to show how smart they were."

– Luke 11:53-54 – As Jesus was leaving, the teachers of religious law and the Pharisees became hostile and tried to provoke

him with many questions. They wanted to trap him into saying
something they could use against him. (NLT)

"People like Judas followed Jesus for money."

> *– John 12:4-6 – But one of his disciples, Judas Iscariot, who*
> *was later to betray him, objected, "Why wasn't this perfume*
> *sold and the money given to the poor? It was worth a year's*
> *wages." He did not say this because he cared about the poor but*
> *because he was a thief; as keeper of the money bag, he used to*
> *help himself to what was put into it.*

"People like the crowd of five thousand followed Jesus for food."

> *– John 6:11-15 – Jesus then took the loaves, gave thanks, and*
> *distributed to those who were seated as much as they wanted.*
> *He did the same with the fish. When they had all had enough to*
> *eat, he said to his disciples, "Gather the pieces that are left over.*
> *Let nothing be wasted." So they gathered them and filled twelve*
> *baskets with the pieces of the five barley loaves left over by*
> *those who had eaten. After the people saw the miraculous sign*
> *that Jesus did, they began to say, "Surely this is the Prophet who*
> *is to come into the world." Jesus, knowing that they intended to*
> *come and make him king by force, withdrew*
> *again to a mountain by Himself.*

"People like the ten lepers followed Jesus for healing."

> *– Luke 17:12-14 – As he was going into a village, ten men with*
> *leprosy came toward him. They stood at a distance and shouted,*
> *"Jesus, Master, have pity on us!" Jesus looked at them and said,*
> *"Go show yourselves to the priests." On their*
> *way they were healed. (CEV)*

"As you can see, many people followed Jesus from a selfish

heart. They cared little for Jesus and more for what He could give them. Today is no different.

As leaders, we should examine ourselves and ask, 'Why am I following Jesus?'

Are you following Jesus so you can become famous?"

"Are you following Him so you can show people how smart you are?

Are you following Jesus for money?

Are you following Him to provide food for your family?

Are you following Jesus with the hope that he will heal you?

People follow Jesus for many reasons. God only blesses one motivation, however. Jesus wants people who follow Him from a heart of love.

Do you remember the outcast sinful woman who poured expensive perfume over Jesus?"

> – Matthew 26:13 – "Truly I say to you, wherever this gospel is preached in the whole world, what this woman has done will also be spoken of in memory of her." (NASB)

"Do you remember the poor widow? Her offering touched Jesus' heart more than all the riches of the temple."

> – Luke 21:3 – "I tell you the truth," Jesus said, "this poor widow has given more than all the rest of them." (NLT)

"Do you remember the one question Jesus asked Peter after he betrayed Him?"

– John 21:17 – The third time he said to him, "Simon son of John, do you love me?" Peter was hurt because Jesus asked him the third time, "Do you love me?" He said, "Lord, you know all things; you know that I love you." Jesus said, "Feed my sheep."

"Jesus questioned Peter about the love in his heart because that is the critical issue for Jesus. Are we following Him because we love Him?

We follow Jesus from a heart of love because He first loved us. We grow strong in God because we love Jesus. We share the gospel because we love Jesus. We make disciples because we love Jesus. We start groups that become churches because we love Jesus. We train spiritual leaders because we love Jesus. Only faith, hope, and love will remain w this earth passes away. The greatest of these, though, is love."

JESUS PLAN PRESENTATIONS

Divide the learners into groups of about eight people each. Explain the following presentation program to leaders.

Leaders form a circle and take turns presenting their "Jesus Plan" to their group. After the presentation, the other leaders lay hands on the "Jesus Plan" and pray for God's power and blessing. Leaders pray aloud at the same time for the leader who presented their plan.

One of the leaders closes the prayer time as the Spirit leads. At that point, the person presenting their "Jesus Plan" holds it to their heart and the group says, "Take up your cross and follow Jesus" three times in unison

Repeat the steps outlined above until every leader has presented their "Jesus Plan."

After everyone presents their plan, leaders join any group not finished. Finally, every group has joined with another until there is only one large group.

End the training time singing a dedication worship song that is meaningful to learners in the group.

THANK YOU

Before you go, I'd like to say "thank you" again for purchasing this book and I hope you have been blessed by it. I know you could have picked from dozens of books, but you felt the Lord leading you to mine.

Again, a big thank you for downloading *Training Radical Leaders* and reading it to the end.

Could I ask a *small* favor? Please take a minute to leave a review for this book on Amazon?

Think of your brief review as giving a short testimony that helps others know if this book is what they need to grow in their spiritual life. Click Here to Leave a Review

Your review will help me continue to write books that help people grow in their walk with Jesus. And if you loved it, please let me know that too! :>

BONUSES

Don't forget to download the special bonuses I have included with this book!

The free *Making Disciples Bonus Pak* which includes three resources to help you pray powerful prayers:

- *100 Promises Audio Version*
- *40 Discipleship Quotes*
- *40 Powerful Prayers*

All are suitable for framing. To download your free *Making Disciples Bonus Pak*, CLICK HERE

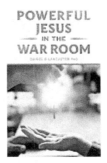

I've also included an excerpt from my bestselling book *Powerful Jesus in the War Room*. God has blessed many through this book and I wanted to give you a chance to "try before you buy." To order *Powerful Jesus in the War Room*, CLICK HERE.

POWERFUL JESUS IN THE WAR ROOM

INTRODUCTION

> Grant Lord, that I may know myself that I may know Thee.
> —Augustine of Hippo —

In this broken world, it is hard for people to accept themselves. Because people don't accept themselves, it is hard to love others too—with a deep love that transforms people, the love others need to feel. If you are like me, you want acceptance and love to permeate your life, but it is hard to come by. Just saying. A friend of mine told me "hurting people hurt people" and I've found that to be so true in my life. The problem is . . . all of us are hurting people. Almost twenty years ago, my wife and I started on a journey of spiritual growth based on eight pictures of Jesus. A picture is worth a thousand words and we discovered that God had given us pictures in the Bible to help us become more like Jesus. Sounds simple and it can be. I'm going to show you how to grow in Christ.

In the process, you will discover how to accept yourself and love others like you never thought possible. If you have read my previous books, you know I don't share theories—just practical action plans that have worked in my life and the lives of many others.

I'm excited you chose this book because I know it is going to change your life. The lessons I am going to share with you have been life-changing for my family, my co-workers, many others, and me. The solutions were developed while our family started two churches in America and refined further as we trained 5,000 nationals in Southeast Asia as missionaries. I've seen people's lives changed repeatedly. I look forward to hearing from you when God does the same in your life.

So, in this book I'm going to share the eight main pictures of Jesus in the Bible. Jesus fulfilled each of these eight pictures completely and perfectly. God has made people in such a way that they are usually strong in two of the pictures but need other pictures to complete them.

This book will teach you why people experience conflict and how you can bring people into unity as a peacemaker. It will look at each of the pictures through the lens of living in the Spirit, from a neutral point of view, or living in the flesh. I will show you a path of spiritual growth that the Lord takes people through as they become more Christlike. When you understand this path, the journey becomes more automatic and less stressful.

My wife and I used these eight pictures of Jesus in our parenting. Raising three boys and one girl is no small task. When we had our first son, it was easy because it was double coverage (to use a football defense analogy). We moved to man-on-man coverage with the birth of our second son. With the birth of our precious daughter, we had to go to zone defense. I remember when our fourth child, a son, came into the world. We moved to prevent defense. Just don't let them score, baby, don't let them score.

Seriously, the eight pictures of Jesus allowed us to raise

passionate, spiritual leaders and bring healing to the nations. We cooperated with what God was doing, rather than trying to figure out our own plans. Each child had strengths in a different picture of Jesus. The tool I'm going to share with you allowed my wife and me to raise a family filled with faith, hope, and love. By God's grace, each of our children has continued as a passionate, spiritual leader to bring healing to the nations.

No one is perfect, but God is good; becoming more like Jesus is a gift he gives those who follow him. After reading this book, you will have the tools you will need to accept yourself, love others, resolve conflicts, and help your family, co-workers, church family, or community experience the healing power of God's love.

In the next chapter, I'm going to show you how to accept yourself. Before you turn the page, however, let me pray.

Lord Jesus,

Thank you for my friend. Thank you for bringing us together in a conversation that changed my life and will change theirs as they read this book.

In your wisdom, you have connected us and will bless as we journey through this book together.

Lord, I'm going to learn even more about you as I write, and I thank you for that. You are so good.

You love us and transform our brokenness.

Thank you.

Lord, my friend is going to learn more about you and a simple way to grow in self-acceptance and love. You know I have struggled with my self-image and how difficult it makes living life sometimes.

Set my readers free, precious Jesus, like you set me free. Fill them with faith, hope, and love for this journey.

May they feel you holding them so very, very close.

Please anoint my words, holy Jesus. This book means little if my friend doesn't fall more in love with you as they read.

In your name. Amen

CHAPTER 1 – WHO AM I?

God loves you just the way you are, but He refuses to leave you that way. He wants you to be just like Jesus.
— Max Lucado —

The biggest barrier to accepting yourself is not understanding how God has made you. When you don't understand the masterpiece, He is making in you, you may get down on yourself and wish you were like "so-and-so." Comparing yourself with others will always lead to not accepting yourself.

In this section, I'm going to show you how to identify which of the eight main personality types God has designed you to be. God made you a certain way and wants you to discover your purpose. Understanding your personality type will give you a deep self-acceptance not affected by circumstances

My parents divorced when I was fifteen and it wasn't pretty.

As a result, I struggled for years with my self-image and self-acceptance. It wasn't until God showed me how he had made me and how much he accepted and loved me that I began to heal. If you find yourself at a similar place, I pray God will use the truths in this book to heal you, too.

As you work through the following exercise, pay attention to what God is speaking deep in your soul. Open your heart to the Holy Spirit. You can discover which of the eight personality types you are in fewer than three minutes and it doesn't cost a dime. What you learn, however, will begin transforming you from the inside out.

So, let's start on the journey. Let me help you find the real you. By the way, doing this exercise with friends and family will make for a very entertaining evening!

Finding Yourself

Start by taking a blank sheet of paper and a pencil. That's all you will need to discover your personality type.

Draw a big circle in the middle of the sheet of paper. The circle represents the whole world and every person living on it. You can find the eight personalities throughout the world in every country and culture.

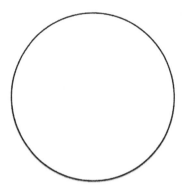

Next, draw a line from left to right and cut the circle in half. On the left side of the circle write the word "task" and on the right side of the circle write the word "people." Draw a short, vertical line to cut the line in half like the picture on the next page.

The world has two basic types of people: task-oriented and people-oriented. The horizontal line represents all those people. Task-oriented people say, "Let's get the work done and then we will play." People-oriented people say, "Let's figure out a way to make this work fun."

Put a dot on the line at the place that best represents the person you are. Before you choose, though, let me make a few comments about this line. First, after God created humanity, He said, "It is good." Wherever you placed yourself on the line—more task-oriented or relationship-oriented—is good. God has created you in a certain way for his glory.

Second, every person has "task" and "people" qualities within them. The line shows which one you stress more. If you are on the "task" side, it doesn't mean you don't care about people, and the other way around. People can care a great deal for others and be task-oriented. People-oriented people can still get the job done.

The last direction I'll give is you can't choose the middle. Sorry. I know you may be half-and-half, but please pick one side or the other. I feel your pain because I have the same trouble.

Okay. It's time to decide where you are on the circle. I have drawn a dot on the task/people line as an example of how a person slightly more task-oriented would choose.

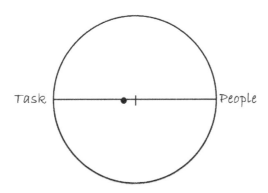

Now, draw a line from the top of the circle to the bottom, making four parts. Label the top of the circle as "extrovert" and the bottom "introvert."

Every person in the world also falls into one of two additional groups: outward-oriented or inward-oriented. Neither group is better than the other one. This is just the way God made people.

Extroverts know many people a little and draw energy from relating with other people. Introverts know a few people well and derive their energy from being alone. If you "never met a stranger," you are an extrovert. If you "think carefully before you speak," you are an introvert.

Choose a point on the extrovert/introvert line that best represents the real you. If you are very outgoing, pick near the top of the circle. If you are private, choose near the bottom of the circle. Again, you can't select the middle. You'll see why in a second.

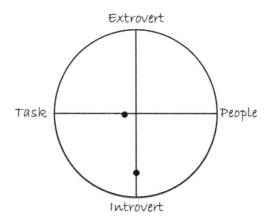

The next step is to discover where on the circle your two marks intersect. Look at the diagram to see what I'm describing as I give you the instructions.

Draw a dotted line from the dot you drew on the task/people

parallel to the extrovert/introvert line until you are right across from your extrovert/introvert dot.

Then, draw a dotted line across from the extrovert/introvert line until you meet the first dotted line you created. Put a star where they come together. This star will help you discover which of the eight personality types you are in a few moments.

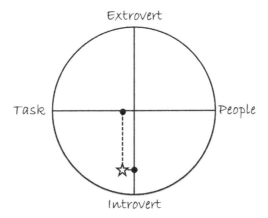

The final step before we talk about the eight personality types is to draw two diagonal lines (an "X") across the circle.

Your circle should now have eight equal pieces and look a little bit like a pizza. Here is a diagram to help you complete this step:

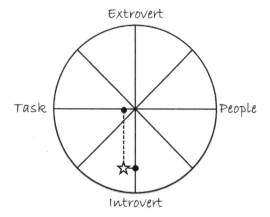

Congratulations! You now have a simple diagram that represents the world with eight different personality types. Now, let's look at short descriptions of each personality type. I'll give you a thumbnail sketch of each one so you can compare the diagram with your own experience. Feel free to read the description of the personality type where your star falls. Then, read the descriptions of the different personality types of people in your life.

To purchase *Powerful Jesus in the War Room* on Amazon CLICK HERE.

BOOKS BY THE AUTHOR

Battle Plan for Prayer Series

Powerful Prayers in the War Room equips you to become a powerful prayer warrior and bring healing and hope to your family and friends. Perfect for small group Bible study.

Powerful Worship in the War Room teaches groups of believers – family or friends – a powerful and practical way to obey the Great Commandment together.

Powerful Jesus in the War Room will strengthen your prayer life by showing you how to connect your personality to one of the eight love languages of Jesus.

Powerful Promises in the War Room is a collection of 100 promises to hide in your heart and defeat Satan in spiritual warfare.

Follow Jesus Training Series

Making Radical Disciples: How to Make Disciples who Multiply Disciples Using Ten Easy-To-Teach Christ-Centered Discipleship Lessons.

Training Radical Leaders: How to Equip Leaders who Develop Leaders Using Ten Christ-Centered Leadership Bible Studies

Starting Radical Churches: How to Start A House Church that Starts New House Churches Using Ten Christ-Centered Church Planting Bible Studies.

Christian Self-Help Guides

Fear is a Liar: How to Stop Anxious Thoughts and Feel God's Love Again. Perfect for Small Group Bible Study.

Shame is a Liar: How to Find Inner Healing and Strength Every Day *(March 2020)*

ABOUT THE AUTHOR

Daniel B Lancaster (PhD) enjoys training others to become passionate followers of Christ. He has planted two churches in America and trained over 5,000 people in Southeast Asia as a strategy coordinator with the *International Mission Board*. He served as Assistant Vice-President for University Ministries at *Union University* and currently is a international missionary with *Cornerstone International*. He has four grown children and a delightful grandson.

Dr. Dan is available for speaking and training events. Contact him at dan@lightkeeperbooks.com to arrange a meeting for your group. All his books are available on Amazon.com.

Made in the USA
Coppell, TX
03 December 2020

42613223R00105